THE ROAD AHEAD

BY

WILLIE HANDLER

ISBN: 978-0-9952945-0-9

This is a work of fiction. Names, characters, places and incidents are the product of the author's imagination or are used fictitiously. Any resemblance to actual persons, living or dead, is entirely coincidental.

Printed in the United States of America.

For Mary Anne for her unwavering love, support and devotion.

TABLE OF CONTENTS

TABLE OF CONTENTS

CHAPTER 1

"Politics is the art of looking for trouble, finding it everywhere, diagnosing it incorrectly and applying the wrong remedies." Groucho Marx

"I've been thinking."

Lois sighs as she sets down a plate of bacon and eggs in front of her husband. "Rick Tompkins, every time you say 'I've been thinking,' I get nervous."

"Hey, that's not fair. You make it sound like I'm some kind of whack job."

"What about the time you decided to build a backyard hockey rink and then come spring, the basement was flooded?"

"We also had heavy rain for a week. It had nothing to do with the rink."

"And what about the time you decided to make your own beer and the bottles exploded in the basement?"

"I knew you would bring that up."

"And there was the time..."

"Okay, already. But this isn't anything like those other things"

She watches her husband pick at his breakfast. "So what's on your mind?"

"The insurance business isn't what it used to be."

She lets out a heavy sigh. "Oh my god. We've had this

conversation before."

"Yeah, I know. Look, when my dad ran Gore General Insurance, it was one of the larger independent brokerage firms in Brampton. I just heard the other day that Dan Mays sold his firm. There are fewer and fewer independents left in town. The competition from direct writers is eating away at my client base."

"You know that existed even when your dad was still involved in the business."

"For sure. Don't get me wrong: we still have a solid client base."

"Then what is it?"

"The thought of keeping the business going for another twenty years or more is stressing me out. There are a lot of changes coming. You know that Google driverless car riding around California?"

"Yes. What about it?"

"Well if the Google car takes off, it could really change the auto insurance market. Maybe people won't need auto insurance anymore, if cars don't run into each other. That's a big chunk of my business. It just puts even more pressure on me to keep building my other insurance lines."

"That isn't going happen for a long time. You have lots of time to adapt."

"And the customers make me crazy. Everyone is pissed off because their auto insurance rates are so high. Like it's my fault that Brampton has the highest rates in Canada. I just don't see myself doing the same thing for forty years."

"Well, I'm sure over time you will figure it out." This is the line she always gives him when he begins to whine about work.

Rick looks up at the clock in the kitchen. "Oh god, I'm going to be late for my golf game." He gets up and drains what's left in his coffee mug. "What are the boys doing today?"

"Jeremy has basketball today. Kyle is going to a movie with two friends."

"Sounds good. I'll call you when I'm on my way home."

———

"You should consider running for office," says Peter, as he leans on his club. "Rick Tompkins signs plastered all over town would be good for your business."

Rick has never considered politics. In fact, Rick doesn't even follow politics. His old university buddy, Peter Lysiak, is now leader of the Ontario Progressive Conservative Party, but they never talk politics when they get together. Peter has been so busy with politics that in the past few years, they haven't seen each other beyond their annual golf day at Glen Abbey in Oakville. This year, they are fortunate to have picked such a gorgeous morning for late May. So when Peter mentions running, as they walk off the tenth green, Rick doesn't even respond.

But the suggestion starts bouncing around in his head. As he thinks about it, using an election campaign to promote his business sounds inspired. As he drives their golf cart to the eleventh tee, he turns to Peter and asks: "What would running for office involve?"

"Let's talk about it in the clubhouse over beer when we're done. I'll give you the lowdown and you can tell me what you think. Right now, you need to concentrate on your game," laughs Peter. "For someone who plays so much, I'd expect you to be a tour player by now. Instead, you're three strokes behind me."

"Don't you worry. We still have eight holes to play."

They are on the fairway of the eleventh hole, not far from each other. To make par, the next shot has to clear Sixteen Mile

Creek which carves the fairway into two parts. The green looks tiny from where they are standing. Peter uses a 7-iron and makes a perfect shot to the back of the green, just short of a row of tall red maple trees behind the hole. Rick also pulls the 7-iron out of his bag. Peter warns him: "You're going to be short and land in the water."

Rick ignores the advice and sure enough, the ball doesn't carry far enough. It hits the bank on the far side of the creek and bounces back into the murky water. He stares at the creek with a pained look on his face. If only that damn greedy creek would spit his ball back onto the green. Peter pats his friend on the shoulder and suggests: "Just drop your ball on the green." Again, Rick ignores him and drops a new ball on the fairway, right in front of the creek. He decides to use his 9-iron and chip it over the water. Unfortunately, he swings too hard and the ball sails past the green. It makes a rustling sound as it passes through the dense group of maple trees and then disappears for good. Angry, Rick slams his club on the ground. It bounces off the spongy turf, pulls out of his hands and lands in the creek. He stares in disbelief at the hideous brown water that has swallowed his $130 custom-fitted club.

Rick's troubles continue. On the thirteenth, he overshoots the green and his ball lands right next to the green on the sixteenth hole. He drives the cart over to his ball and gets out of the cart to make his next shot. He takes a glance behind him and sees only an empty fairway and blue sky. As he begins his back swing, he hears a *thunk* as a ball bounces off his cart. He turns around and yells. "Hey asshole! You're supposed to yell fore!"

A middle-aged Asian man pulls up in a cart. "I'm terribly sorry. I didn't see you there. Are you alright?"

"I can't believe you people. You drive golf balls as bad as you drive cars."

"I beg your pardon? That is a terrible and unfair stereotype."

"I work in the insurance industry and believe me, it's no stereotype."

The golfer approaches Rick with an iron in his hand. His face is as red as a rare piece of meat. "There's no place in Canada for bigots like you."

Rick grabs his oversized driver for protection. "Horseshit. What do you know about being Canadian? My family's been in Canada for over a hundred years." Both men are eyeing the other and waving their clubs in the air.

Peter arrives just in time to prevent a modern version of jousting from breaking out. He pulls the two apart and drags Rick back to the cart. "Rick, try to remember I'm a member here. You can't be getting into altercations with other golfers."

By the eighteenth hole, Rick is a broken man. The hole is a short par five and he is tempted to try to get on the green in two shots but there is a water hazard the size of a lake in front of the green and large bunkers behind it. As he lines up his second shot, he remembers how in the 2000 Canadian Open, Tiger Woods had made an incredible 218-yard, 6-iron shot from a fairway bunker over the water and onto the back fringe of the green. He sighs. He then takes aim for the front of the water acknowledging that making par would at least allow him to finish the day with some dignity.

Peter finishes the game with a respectable eighty-eight on what is a challenging course. Rick finishes with a score over a hundred, and a bag that is considerably lighter with a 9-iron at the bottom of the creek, a bent driver left at the fourteenth and eleven balls sucked up by the water hazards and the trees.

As they head into *Eighteen at Glen Abbey*, the clubhouse restaurant, Peter reminds him: "You do still remember that the loser buys drinks?"

"Go ahead and rub it in."

They are seated at a table right by the windows, which overlook the eighteenth green. The fairway looks like a lush green carpet that is broken up by two odd-shaped sand traps and a large water hazard. The sky is virtually cloudless and the sun is still well above the treetops that border the fairway. The bright light makes it necessary for them to position their chairs so the sun isn't directly in their eyes. While perusing the menu, Peter decides to return to his earlier question. "So what do you think about my idea of running for office?"

"It's not something I've ever been interested in. You're the *pol*, not me."

As far back as Rick can remember, Peter has always been involved in politics. When they attended McMaster University in Hamilton back in the late 1980s, Peter had been active with the PC Youth and president of the Student Union in their final year. They belonged to the Pi Kappa Alpha fraternity, where Rick distinguished himself for his drinking. The 'frat brothers' became very close and, over the years, have been there for each other. They served as best man for each other when they got married. After graduating Peter became involved with several Oakville candidates while working in the family construction business. He joined the political staff of a Conservative MPP following the 1996 election. He eventually ran for the Conservatives in 2004 and won a seat representing Oakville. After a dreadful election campaign in 2008 in which the Conservatives finished third, the party leader resigned and Peter ran an inspired leadership bid. It didn't hurt his chances that the party was demoralized after so many senior MPPs were defeated and most veteran caucus members decided to pass on the leadership race. Always the opportunist, Peter won the leadership with the promise to rebuild the party.

Rick adds: "But humor me, what do you have in mind?"

"It's been forever since the Conservatives have won a seat in Brampton although way back when, we did have a premier from Brampton. There aren't a lot of Conservatives in Bramalea-Gore-Malton and we're having a hell of a time coming up with a candidate for the election this fall."

"Good Lord, you want me to run in Bramladesh?"

"Rick, it's your hometown," responds Peter disapprovingly shaking his head. "I can't believe you refer to your own city using that derogatory term."

"Peter, it's the brownest place in Canada. I think I'm actually a minority in Brampton. Why don't you find yourself someone named Kumar or Sunil to run? Won't that increase your chance of winning?"

"I'm well aware that white voters are a minority in the riding. My staff keep me informed on riding demographics. We don't actually expect to win the riding this time around. I hope, if we have some success in the election, we can build on that and begin recruiting some stronger candidates in the future, in particular, from the ethnic communities. Right now, I just need someone to raise the Conservative flag in the riding for six weeks. As a friend, local resident, and business person, I thought I would approach you first."

"I get it. Though I find it hard to believe I'm the first person you approached to run in the riding. I may not be into politics but I didn't just arrive here from Mars. There aren't a lot of voters who call themselves Conservatives in Brampton. Now excuse me for sounding a little crass but what's in it for me?" Rick knows what the answer will be but he feels a need to ask anyway.

"I know you are not the least bit interested in politics but you do run a business in town. A campaign gets you out in the community with an opportunity to meet new people who might potentially become new clients. Look at it as a unique marketing opportunity. It's a win-win for both of us."

"Okay, let's say I'm interested. I don't know the first thing about running an election campaign. I wouldn't know where to start."

"First off, we need to get you nominated. That might not be a problem since you might end up being the only candidate seeking the nomination. I will parachute in some people to organize things for you. I'll even send you Jerry Switzer who is a crack policy person from my office."

The server drops by the table to see if they want more drinks. Rick asks for the check. He turns back to Peter. "I think I can manage the time. I've got brokers in the office that can cover for me. But I want to speak to Lois first before I commit."

As they head out the door to the parking lot, Peter shakes his friend's hand. "That was lots of fun as always. It was good to see you. Call me in the morning and let me know what you think."

CHAPTER 2

"Under every stone lurks a politician." Aristophanes

The drive from Glen Abbey to the Castlemore neighborhood in northwest Brampton is about fifty kilometers. It can take anywhere from forty-five minutes to over an hour depending on the roads, which are chronically congested with impatient and aggressive drivers. That stereotype about Canadians being so nice? It doesn't exist on the roads and highways around Toronto and its suburbs. Think Mad Max but at lower speeds. Rick is the poster boy for road rage. Anyone driving slower than him is inevitably called a moron and anyone driving faster is a maniac.

Rick pulls onto the 407 electronic toll highway, which usually has much lighter traffic because of the ridiculously high tolls. Once he gets off the highway, it's less than ten kilometres home. He hopes that the final leg will be problem free. However, as he exits the 407 onto Airport Road, his car becomes entangled in a classic Brampton traffic jam.

Rick pulls out his phone to check for emails and messages. As he scrolls through the messages, he determines there is nothing important that needs his attention. He calls Lois.

"How was your game?"

"I don't want to talk about it."

"You always play poorly with Peter. If you ask me, he intimidates you."

"I didn't ask you."

"So grumpy today. How's Peter doing?"

"He's fine. I just called to let you know I'm on my way home. There's something I want to get your advice on. Sorry if I'm sounding so cryptic. We can talk when I get home."

"Sure. I'll wait for my mystery man to show up. Bye."

The Castlemore neighborhood is your typical upper-middle class suburban subdivision. Street after street of identical 3,000 square foot homes and perfect lawns, with a park thrown in every few blocks. You could easily pull into the wrong driveway if you aren't paying attention. Rick has done that on a few occasions. When he arrives home, Rick opens the garage door with his car remote and takes his clubs out of the trunk to store in the back of the garage. He uses the garage entrance which leads into the laundry room and moments later strolls into the kitchen where Lois is preparing dinner. He pauses to watch her. His wife is in her forties but clearly not showing her age. Her raven black hair shows no sign of grey and not because of any intervention by her hair salon.

When she turns around, she notices him in the room. "Would you like something cold to drink?"

"Thanks, I can get it myself." Rick walks over to the fridge and pulls out a bottle of beer. He opens it and gulps down half the bottle.

"So tell me what's up?" Rick and Lois have been married for seventeen years but have known each other for over twenty. The fact that Rick wasn't his chatty self on the phone means he has something on his mind. "Don't tell me that you've done something embarrassing at Glen Abbey. Hopefully not because that could get back to my dad. He doesn't need another reason to dislike you."

Lois' father, Don Brand is very much old school. He operates a farm in Caledon, Ontario that has been in the family since the early 1900s. Don's grandfather emigrated from Germany and settled in the farm community north of Toronto to raise cattle. Don's Heritage Farm exclusively raises cattle that are free of growth hormones and drugs. Heritage Farm is well known for its superior quality beef and Don has purchased Angus cattle from Scotland, Charolais cattle from France and Wagyu cattle from Japan. Wagyu beef is sold at about $100 per pound and has put Heritage Farm "designer" beef products on the same status as Moët & Chandon champagne, Oakley sunglasses and Prada handbags.

Rick lets out a sigh. "Oh yes, we don't want to upset your father." Don has always made it clear to Rick that he would have wanted his daughter to have found someone better. Over the years, Don has labelled him as loud, abrasive, lazy, familiar, opinionated and ill-mannered. Rick often feels that Lois married him as a way of rebelling against her father. Much like her father, she doesn't hesitate to chew him out when she feels he is being brash or insensitive. Yet, she has stood by him all these years. He tells people how she was never that serious about him until she had to undergo emergency surgery for a burst appendix. Rick showed up at the hospital every day, bringing her little gifts. Eventually, she fell for him.

"Rick, you know my father is very set in his ways. It is what it is."

"It's very frustrating. I don't think there is anything he likes about me."

"I don't think that's necessarily true."

"It's true. He feels I'm not ambitious because I was handed the insurance business by my father and uncle. But I think I've worked hard to sustain the business. It's tough out there."

"It's sad that after seventeen years of marriage, not much of a bond exists between you and Dad. But all that matters is that I love you." She gives him a peck on the cheek.

"I know."

"So tell me what you talked to Peter about."

"He asked me to run for office in the next provincial election"

"Really? What was your answer?"

"I said I would think about it."

"I thought you hated politics."

"I wouldn't say that I hate it. More like I'm disinterested."

"Then why are you thinking about it?"

"It's like this. I wouldn't necessarily be running to win. In fact, you can pretty much count on me losing. After all, I'd be running in Brampton and no one votes Conservative in Brampton."

"So what's the point?"

"Whether or not the riding is winnable, Peter needs someone on the ballot. So he asked me. He gets a candidate for five or six weeks while I get to meet a lot of people, some of whom may also happen to have insurance needs. When it's all over, I go back to my insurance business with a bunch of new contacts and he heads back to Queen's Park. Maybe as Premier."

"What happens if you win?"

"I'm not going to win. Do you think Peter would ask me if he thought there was a chance of winning this riding? We may be good friends but I doubt he wants me sitting in the legislature with him."

"Well it sounds like you've made up your mind. For the record, I'm okay with whatever you decide. Just be prepared for the worst," she says with a laugh. "Four years as an MPP."

Rick puts down his empty beer bottle and embraces his wife. He whispers in her ear: "So the worst case scenario is I'll get in and do something good for the community, like getting the Spadina subway line extended to Brampton."

She pulls away and playfully slaps him on the arm. "That's a stupid idea," she says as she laughs, "which is why you'd make a great politician."

"Well if I win, I'll come up with some better ones. I'll call Peter in the morning."

———————

The first thing that Rick typically does on Monday mornings is check his personal email and phone messages. Most are requests for insurance quotes and there are usually a few clients who have had collisions over the weekend. Rick hands over some of the quote requests to his customer service representative for follow up.

Gore General Insurance is located on Queen Street near the intersection with Main Street, in downtown Brampton. The firm has six registered independent brokers and a total staff of fourteen. It was started in 1965 by his father, Malcolm Tompkins, and his Uncle Bruce, who have both since retired and handed over the reins to Rick.

For years now, Brampton has been plagued with a high number of auto-related insurance claims and fraud. The area has the dubious distinction of having the highest auto insurance rates in Canada. Rick and the other brokers need to keep a careful eye on their book of business, which means careful screening of new clients. Should their book of business incur too many claims, they risk having one of the insurance companies they deal with cancel their agency contract. To mitigate this risk, Rick will call some clients who have had an accident to determine if it is a minor fender bender. If the client is at fault, he will suggest that the client pay for the repairs to both of the damaged cars and not report the accident to the two insurance companies. The rationale he provides is that the client's premium will increase considerably following a claim. But really, he just wants to keep the number of claims attributed to Gore's clients low and not put the firm at risk.

He notices one message is from a client, Gary Bloduin, who is reporting an accident. Gary had a claim last year and a second claim would put him in a high-risk category. He picks up the phone. "Good morning Gary, it's Rick."

"Hi Rick, thanks for calling back. My wife backed into someone at Bramalea City Centre yesterday."

"Well, let's see if we can avoid putting a claim through. Your premium is about $240 a month right now on that car. If you put through a claim, it will probably go up to about $600 a month or more."

"What? That's crazy! It was just some minor damage."

"Insurers rate you by the number of claims and not by the size of the claim. You had one last year so you would be considered a higher risk. How much damage is there to the two cars?"

"My car has some scrapes to the bumper. I can live with them. The other car probably has about $1500 in damages."

"Who did you hit? Was it a car full of brown people? Because they'll be running to a paralegal to cash in on your little fender bender."

"No, nothing like that. It was some older woman in a low-end Ford."

"My advice is call her up and offer to pay for the damages and even a rental while it's getting repaired. The $2,000 it will cost you will be less than your increased premiums, just in the first year."

"Thanks Rick. By the way, do you have a thing against Asian people?"

"Hey I have nothing but love for those people. But there are a lot of immigrants getting sucked into schemes to make some quick cash off of insurance companies. Let me know what happens."

After returning a few more calls, Rick decides to call Peter. He calls Peter's cell phone and a woman's voice answers. "Geneva Horvath, how can I help you?"

"Who are you?"

"Peter Lysiak's chief of staff."

"I'm Rick Tompkins, I'm trying to reach Peter."

"I'm sure I can help you Mr. Tompkins."

"I don't need help, I just need to speak to Peter."

"Let me explain how this works, Mr. Tompkins. The job of the chief of staff is to control access to the boss. That's what I'm paid to do. So if you want access, you need to tell me what it's about. If it's personal, I still need to hear about it. If you are selling magazine subscriptions, well I decide what he reads. If you are a *Toronto Star* reporter, I can tell you what Peter is thinking. If you are his wife calling to ask that he bring home a carton of milk, I'll arrange to get you the milk. Do you get the picture?"

"Okay, I got it. Peter asked me about running in the next election."

"Just one moment." With that, she puts Rick on hold.

"Hey Rick, Geneva tells me you've made a decision."

"That woman is such a stuck up bitch. Where did you find her?"

"She can be a hard ass. You need to have a little of that to do the job. I'm glad you're on board. We really appreciate it. So what have you decided?"

"I'm your candidate."

"Marvelous!"

"So what's the next step?"

"I'm going to send over Jerry Switzer to get you organized. He's my Director of Policy and a very sharp guy. He will run the show for you. Geneva will arrange for Jerry to come by to introduce himself and get the ball rolling."

"Thanks Peter. I'll wait for Jerry's call."

About an hour later, Jerry's call gets redirected onto Rick's line. "Hi Rick, I'm Jerry Switzer. I understand from Peter Lysiak that you will be running for the nomination in Bramalea-Gore-Malton and I'll be managing your campaign."

"Welcome aboard Jerry. I'm a rookie so it's your show."

"How about I swing by tomorrow afternoon? I'd like to go over what's involved."

"Tomorrow afternoon works for me. I'm available after 2:00 p.m."

"You're up in Brampton, right?"

"Yes I'm in Brampton, 22 Queen Street East."

"Great, I'll see you then."

CHAPTER 3

"We'd all like to vote for the best man but he's never a candidate." Kim Hubbard

Jerry can hear the sound of his phone vibrating on the nightstand. He can't understand why the thing still makes noise when the ringer is off. Silence should be just that. Without opening his eyes, he rolls over to grab his phone. "Hello?"

"It's your mother calling."

"Hi Mom." He resists the urge to yawn into the phone. "It's 6:05 a.m. Why are you calling this early? Is something wrong?"

"Everything is fine. I just wanted to make sure I caught you in."

"Catch me in? I have a cell phone. You can reach me any time of the day."

"You're so busy that I can never get a hold of you. So I decided to call while you're still home."

"You mean while I'm still sleeping." He can't resist anymore as he yawns into the phone.

"If I don't hear from you, how will I know you're still alive?"

"Spoken like a true Jewish mother. Imagine the worst so that you can always have plenty to worry about. Sorry to disappoint you but everything is fine."

"When will we see you again? Your father and I barely remember what you look like. We have to pull out old photographs to remind us."

"It hasn't been that long. I'll come by for dinner on Friday."

"Will you be bringing someone with you?"

"No Mom, I'm not seeing anyone. I told you I have no time for a social life right now."

"You're thirty-four years old. It's not normal to be single at thirty-four. People will think there's something wrong with you. Like you're a sociopath or retarded."

"You don't call people retarded today. They're called developmentally handicapped."

"Okay, so people will think my Jerry is developmentally handicapped."

"Enough already. Thanks for calling Mom. I have to get ready for work. I'll see you on Friday."

"Goodbye darling."

"Bye."

Jerry is sitting on the edge of his bed rubbing his eyes. He gazes around the tiny 550 square-foot condo and notices how disgusting it has become. There are empty food containers scattered around the apartment. The furniture is best described as post-modern IKEA: nothing matches. Items of clothing are scattered all around and a fine layer of dust on the furniture resembles a street after freshly fallen snow. When did the cleaning company last show up? They're definitely overdue.

He stumbles into the bathroom for a shower. Because he has an outside appointment later in the day to meet the new candidate in Brampton, Jerry decides to put on a suit. There is only one suit hanging in his closet. The big decision is which of his two ties to wear. He looks at himself in the mirror. He knows he looks a little odd. He is short and balding with thick glasses on a nose that overpowers the rest of his face. He has a distinct paunch and his suit doesn't fit properly. His pants are too short and his jacket sleeves are too long. It would be obvious to anyone that he buys off the rack.

Next is a quick stop at Tim Hortons to pick up some breakfast before heading into the office. The lineup to place an order snakes all the way to the door, which is typical for this hour of the morning, and to which Jerry is oblivious because he is preoccupied with his BlackBerry. It takes almost fifteen minutes for Jerry to reach the front of the line. The server recognizes Jerry. "Large coffee with cream and sugar and a toasted poppy seed bagel with cream cheese?" He nods and returns to his BlackBerry until his order is ready.

The Progressive Conservative leader's office is on the third floor of the Legislative Building. Jerry takes the stairs up to the office suite that houses Peter Lysiak, as well as his staff. As Jerry walks down the corridor, he notices Geneva stirring around in her office. He pokes his head in. "Morning."

"Hi Switzer." She always addresses him by his surname because she knows it irritates him even though he tries hard not to show it. She loves to push his buttons.

"Thanks for assigning me to the most unwinnable campaign ever." The sarcasm only makes her smile. "What can you tell me about Rick Tompkins since I'm going to be spending the next few months with this guy?"

"He's a personal friend of Peter's. They were frat brothers or something like that. That's why you're the man. Besides, we also need to breathe some life into the riding association, which is essentially dormant. We'll never win there unless they get better organized."

"I'll do what I can."

"I can tell you that my initial read of this guy is that he has a bit of an attitude. Hopefully, he won't be a problem."

"I'm driving up to Brampton to meet with him today."

"Well, good luck."

––––––––––––––

Jerry pulls his white 2006 Chevrolet Cobalt out of his parking space in his condo building. The dirt on the car and the dim underground lighting makes the car appear grey. He knows it makes no sense to own a car since he rarely drives it but he can't seem to give it up. He can reach most places he needs to by foot and public transit. The rest he could cover by taking cabs or using a car sharing service like Zipcar. Perhaps this will be his last car. The interior has never been cleaned. The back seat has as much paper as his office desk. There is a foul smell, probably from food that has fallen under the front seats. The front windshield has a chip in it that is beginning to spread like a spider web. The car's muffler can't be in good shape because every time he presses down on the accelerator, the noise reminds him of a jet turbine.

Although Jerry has lived in Toronto most of his life, being a downtown person, he has never actually been to Brampton. He isn't quite sure what route to take so pulls out his GPS to make sure it gets him there. He despises the suburbs. Miles of developments with cookie-cutter houses and shopping malls Suburbanites drive everywhere. And their kids are driven everywhere. It's as if they have lost the ability to walk but then again, there isn't anything within walking distance. Everything is situated in malls or even bigger "power centers" with large box stores anchored by a Wal-Mart or Costco store. Every place must have lots of parking, otherwise no one will come.

When he arrives at Brampton's downtown core, he is not in the least impressed. It's too gritty and lifeless for his liking. Queen Street has little pedestrian traffic. Jerry notices a number of homeless men wandering up and down the street. Not what he expected from a city of over half a million people. He circles the block in front of Rick's office several times before he finally finds a parking spot.

Gore General Insurance is sandwiched between a legal office and Bijou Nail Salon and Spa. When Jerry gets to reception, the woman at the desk directs him to Rick's office. Jerry knocks on his door and the person at the desk jumps up to greet him. "Hi, I'm Rick Tompkins. You must be Jerry." Rick's office is quite large considering the size of the space occupied by the firm but appropriate for someone with a slightly oversized ego. The office has large natural oak furniture and leather chairs with lots of comfy stuffing. The credenza behind the desk has several golf and hockey trophies. Above the credenza, on the wall, are plaques from youth hockey and soccer teams that Gore has sponsored over the years. Rick notices Jerry looking at the plaques. "My son, Kyle, played on these teams."

"How old is he?"

"Ten."

"Any other children?"

"I have another son. Jeremy. He's thirteen."

"I'm sure you're very proud of them." Jerry is standing awkwardly in front of Rick's desk when he realizes that Rick isn't going to invite him to sit down. He timidly works his way over to a side chair in front of the desk and slinks into the seat. The man behind the desk is taller than Jerry but under six feet. His brown hair is gelled and combed back. He has a moustache that looks like something between a paintbrush and what you would expect a walrus to be wearing. Below that is a rather unattractive weak chin. He is tanned but a little too orange to be natural. For this time of the year, it has to be a shake'n'bake tan. He is wearing tan slacks and a light blue golf shirt.

"Hmm...Switzer. Are you Jewish? Because there's a Jewish deli in Mississauga called Switzer's."

"Yes, I am Jewish. Is that a problem?"

"Nope. In fact, you people are very successful in politics, aren't you?"

Red flags are waving all over the place in Jerry's head. Is this guy really going to run for office? "Yes, some Jews are politically active. As are other people."

"But Jewish people have political smarts. You know how to win."

At this point, Jerry is tightly gripping the arms of the chair and forcing a smile. "Sorry to disappoint you but those are stereotypes. There are Jewish people who fail at politics, make lousy lawyers and accountants and don't have much money. Nonetheless, I do know how to run a political campaign, which is why I'm here."

"Yeah, yeah. I was just making small talk. By the way do you work with that Geneva?"

"Yes, she's my boss. She runs Peter's office."

"She is one fucking bitch, excuse my French."

"I like to say that Geneva is Conservative Party royalty. Her grandfather was mayor of Galt for many years. Her uncle was an alderman in Galt and, after amalgamation, became a Cambridge councilor. Her brother is currently a Cambridge councilor. All Conservative politicians. Politics runs in her blood. Her resume is a little on the light side but she is no lightweight. She ran a health food store before jumping into politics. She is drop dead gorgeous and knows it. Though I sense there was a time when she might have been an ugly duckling and is trying to make up for it now. Don't cross her because she will cut off your balls. Peter Lysiak needed Horvath family support to win the leadership, which is part of the reason Geneva is his chief of staff. But she is more than just competent."

"Okay. I'll be sure to stay clear of Margaret Thatcher. So what's the plan?"

"Well to start, you need to win the nomination. That shouldn't be a problem since you are likely to go uncontested. There's little interest out there from potential candidates when success is considered drawing more votes than the Green Party. Once you are the official candidate, we can do some fundraising. A good place to start is family and business associates."

"I know my father-in-law has done fundraising for Conservative candidates. I'll see how he feels about helping out."

"That would be great. Maybe with his help we can come up with an event or two to bring in some cash. You need a lot of individual donors. There are limits on how much a donor can contribute to an individual candidate. It's not unusual to have each family member contribute to a candidate. So mom, dad, cousin Joey and grandma can all contribute."

"So what else do we need to do?"

"We will need a campaign office and some furniture. I'll look into renting them for the duration of the campaign. I can scout around for some possibilities. We will also need to round up some volunteers for canvassing, phoning, putting up signs and all the grunt work that goes into a campaign."

"Well, I can't wait to get started. I want to print signs made up with the same colors as my company logo, blue and gold."

"Umm, no can do. The party requires that election signs conform with standard colors and style. The colors are blue and white. It's all about branding."

"I'm just trying to see if I can sneak in my own brand. When the election is over, I'll be back at my day job and it would be great if some of the nice people I meet become clients, if you know what I mean. So what's the first thing we need to do?"

"Let's file nomination papers and then we can raise some money. You can start by hitting up people you know."

"Sure, I'll get right on it."

CHAPTER 4

"Money is like manure. You have to spread it around or it smells." J.P. Getty

On the drive to Heritage Farms, Rick repeatedly goes over what he plans to say to Don. A Bon Jovi CD is blasting away from the car stereo. He checks himself out in the rearview mirror. His brown hair has touches of grey in it and is neatly trimmed, along with his moustache - with a little help from his barber. Yes, he looks polished and confident. Things are going to go just fine. That prick of a father-in-law had better step up.

Rick knows that Don doesn't think he is good enough for Lois. Rick knows nothing about farming and Don is a crusty, old farmer. Surely, he will be supportive of a run for a seat in the Legislature, in particular because he will be running under the Progressive Conservative banner?

Rick is about two kilometers from the farm when he checks himself out in the mirror one more time. As his eyes return to the road, he suddenly notices a raccoon that has run right in front of his car. He swerves to avoid it and his Lincoln Navigator skids off the road into a ditch filled with thick, dark mud. Rick sits staring ahead with adrenaline still rushing through his body when he screams at no one in particular, "Damn raccoons!" He opens the car door to study the situation. As he steps out of the car, his foot sinks and he falls forward into several inches of slimy, smelly mud. The mud is cold and has a faint smell of manure, which makes him gag. He makes several attempts to get up but the weight of the mud clinging to his clothes keeps pulling him down. Finally, he pulls himself up and gazes into the car mirror. All he can make out is a grey pile of muck with two blinking eyes. He gets back behind the wheel and makes several attempts to drive the car out of the ditch. All that he accomplishes is getting mud all over the car's interior. Driving out of the ditch proves to be impossible as the car's tires are unable to get any traction. Reluctantly, he decides the prudent thing to do is call Don and get him to pull his car out with his tractor. He reaches into his jacket pocket for his cell phone. It's not there. He searches through the car but it fails to turn up. It must have fallen out of his pocket when he went head first into the mud. He gets back into the mud on his hands and knees feeling around for his phone. After several minutes, he locates it but the discovery provides no relief from his misery. The muck has killed his phone.

The only option that remains for Rick is to make his way on foot to his in-laws. As he lumbers his way down the road, the hot sun is quickly drying the mud clinging to his clothing. Over time, dried clumps of mud break away leaving a trail behind him. About twenty minutes later, Rick is knocking on his in-laws' door, still covered from head to toe in dried mud. The Brand home is no ordinary farm house. It is an impressive 3,000 square-foot Tudor-style home built out of brick and stucco with a steep gabled roof and tall, narrow leaded glass windows. Don opens the door and stares at Rick for a moment before collecting his thoughts to remark, "Young man, isn't Halloween still months away?" with one eyebrow raised.

Don's wife Sylvia intervenes and leads Rick into the laundry room. "Rick, take those things off and I'll throw them in the washer. Don will bring you something to wear." Several minutes later Don walks into the laundry carrying a pair of jeans and a plaid shirt. When he sees Rick standing awkwardly in his underwear, he breaks into a smirk. "Looks like you've put on a few pounds there."

Rick's face is now a bright crimson. "Umm...thanks for the clothes, Don."

When Rick finishes changing, he walks down the hall to the kitchen where he finds Sylvia making coffee. The large, bright kitchen is decorated colonial-style with white cabinetry and butcher block counters. A plate of homemade scones sit on a round pine table surrounded by straight-backed chairs. "Have a seat and make yourself comfortable. Don will be down in a minute. Help yourself to something to eat. The coffee is just about ready."

"Thanks Sylvia. I love your raisin scones."

Just then Don walks into the room. "Well, what brings you to farm country? You weren't just in the neighborhood." Don pours a cup of coffee and takes a seat at the table.

"I wanted to let you know that I'm seeking the Conservative nomination for the riding of Bramalea-Gore-Malton."

He looks genuinely surprised. "Really? When did you become a Conservative?"

"Peter Lysiak asked me to consider running and I've accepted."

"You aren't going to find very many Conservative voters there."

"I'm doing this to help out Peter and the party. He's having problems finding a candidate."

Don scratches his beard. "I get it. You're taking one for the team so to speak. But you don't know the first thing about politics and campaigning."

"Peter sent over Jerry Switzer to be my campaign manager."

He takes a deep breath. "I could really use your help too."

"I hear Jerry is a sharp guy. You might learn something from him. What type of help are you looking for from me?"

"I am hoping you could organize a fundraiser for me."

"I see. Well I think I can pull something together. I'm always here to help my fellow Conservatives. It's about time you grew up and took life more seriously. Too bad you haven't a hope in hell of winning. But you never know, maybe Brampton will wise up to the 'tax and spend' Liberals."

They chat a while longer. Rick picks up that the public is tiring of the Liberals after ten years in office. According to Don, people are very impressed with Peter Lysiak and his platform. "Ontario is ready for a responsible government that will look after their hard earned dollars. He feels that just about any riding is up for grabs."

"Just not my riding," responds Rick.

"We'll see. You can't really know until voters turn their mind to who they support."

"What do you think voters are looking for?"

"I think the next government needs to be focused on balancing the budget, lowering taxes and job creation." They chat for over an hour. For once, Rick is pleased. This might be the first time they have had something in common.

When Rick's clothes have been washed and dried, Sylvia returns them to Rick. There is still the matter of his car, which remains stuck in mud on the side of the road. Don gets his tractor from behind the barn and Rick hops on the back as they make their way to where Rick had to abandon his car. Don pulls the tractor directly in front of Rick's car. He gets off the tractor and ties one end of a rope to a hitch in the back of the tractor and the other end to the front end of the car. Rick gets into the driver's seat and starts up the car. Don nudges the tractor forward until there is no slack left in the rope. When Don gives him a signal, Rick begins to slowly press down on the accelerator. Don continues to inch the tractor forward which now has the car moving as well. Eventually, the rotating tires find a hard surface and begin to power the car forward. Both vehicles stop on the road. Don gets out and unties the rope. They shake hands and go off in different directions.

CHAPTER 5

**"Politics is perhaps the only profession for which
no preparation is thought necessary."**
Robert Louis Stevenson

The next few weeks are busy for Jerry, as he works on pulling together a campaign from scratch. Because there is no active riding association, there is no election infrastructure to tap into. The first step is securing the nomination. He immediately files papers on behalf of Rick to formalize the process. Although he doesn't anticipate anyone else running for the nomination, he still feels they must sign up new party members who will support Rick in the event the nomination is contested. Jerry drags Rick out with him to knock on doors to find those new members. Rick complains the entire time because it is taking him away from more enjoyable things, such as playing golf and spending time at the cottage.

Don Brand comes through for Rick by tapping into his contact list of generous Conservative supporters. Jerry reaches out to a York University student who is active with the Ontario PC Youth Association to set up and maintain a website and social media feed for Rick.

When July comes around, they have signed up over 400 new members and the party announces the date of the riding nomination meeting. Still no one else, other than Rick, has filed for the nomination. The nomination meeting is held on a humid Thursday evening in late July. Just under a hundred people show up in the gym at St. Rita Elementary School to show their support and enjoy the free food provided by the campaign.

Jerry has prepared a short speech for Rick. The message is consistent with the party's policy book. The speech is laced with goodies like "Ontario has had enough of tax and spend governments" and "only Conservatives respect the public's pocketbook." Some in the audience actually stopped scarfing down the free pizza and pasta to listen to Rick. Jerry noticed a couple of reporters present from the *Brampton Guardian* and *Mississauga News* but no one from one of the major Toronto papers. Of course, why would they?

There are over 100,000 eligible voters in Bramalea-Gore-Malton — or, as Jerry likes to refer to it: BGM. But there are fewer than 50,000 residents who ever vote. Jerry digs up the results of the past three elections and discovers that no previous Progressive Conservative candidate received more than 6,000 votes. He concludes even if they were to triple that amount, it might still not be enough to win an election. Despite a guaranteed loss, he feels it is still his duty to attract as many voters as possible to the party and build a base for the next election.

The morning after the nomination meeting, Jerry checks out potential locations for a campaign office. The ideal location would be on a major street with considerable visibility and foot traffic. On day three of his search, Jerry finds an acceptable location. It is a cavernous space that used to be a bible school and, prior to that, a supermarket. He works out a great deal with the owner who is happy to find a short-term tenant while he is looking for a buyer for the property.

Jerry has rounded up a group of campaign volunteers using the list of party members they had signed up in the previous

weeks. In addition, Jerry is able to locate old lists ⟨
from previous campaigns. He arranges for a me⟨
home on a weeknight evening following the Civic ⟨⟩
early August. Jerry arrives shortly before the start of the meeti⟨⟩
Moments after ringing the bell, the door swings open and Lois
greets him. "Good evening Jerry."

He awkwardly stretches out his hand in order to shake hers.
"Nice to see you, Lois."

She grabs it and pulls him into the house. "Everyone is in the
dining room. Follow me." She leads him into a dining room with a
ten-foot table and about a dozen chairs squeezed around it. Rick is
seated at the head of the table and to his right are two young women
in their early twenties. As Jerry enters the room, they all stand up to
greet him. One of the women is a tall, slender blonde with brilliant
blue eyes and long legs. She is wearing stiletto heels which make her
appear giraffe-like when she takes a step. Her tight, black skirt ends
well above her knees. The finishing touch is a sheer white blouse
partly covered by a pink, lacy sweater. The other woman is shorter
and very shapely. Her walk resembles that of a panther, nimble
and fluid. She has large, brown eyes and red hair that falls past her
shoulders and to just above her generous bosom. She is wearing
a similar skirt in green and a sweater that exposes a considerable
amount of cleavage.

Rick steps forward to do the introductions. "This is Jerry,
the guy I told you about. He's going to be our campaign manager
or, as I refer to him, the election genius. This is Ginny." The tall
blonde sticks out her hand to Jerry. "And this is Brittney." The
redhead does a half wave. "The girls work in my office and want
to volunteer for the campaign."

The doorbell rings. Lois leads in a petite Indian woman
who appears to be in her late twenties. Jerry rushes to greet her.
"Hey I'm glad you made it! Rick, let me introduce you to your

.nunications coordinator, Ameena 3 Gupta."

Rick extends his hand out to greet her. "Nice meeting you, meena."

"I go by Ameena 3."

"What do you mean, like Ameena the third?"

"No, my middle name is 3."

"That's pretty queer. Why did your parents give you a number for a middle name?"

"They never provided me with a middle name. When I was a teenager, I decided to take on 3 as my middle name. I'm very much into Indian numerology. People who are associated with the number 3 are truly optimistic from the core. They look at everything with a positive vision and find everything positive in their surroundings. They will see something good even in the worst possible event. Their immense optimism is their strength, but it could also be their weakness, at times."

Rick rolls his eyes. "Okay, I gotcha. It's Ameena 3."

Jerry jumps in. "Not only is Ameena 3 a great writer but she is also fluent in Punjabi. She will definitely be an asset for the campaign."

Jerry grabs Ameena 3 by the arm and pulls her into another room. "I just want to give you a heads up. Rick is not exactly politically correct."

Her eyebrows are raised and her nose is scrunched up. "Oh? Like what are we talking about here?"

"Well, for example, he keeps talking about the brown people in the riding."

"Come on Jerry. I didn't sign up for this kind of bullshit."

"Look, if you stick it out to the end, I'll speak to Geneva and get you a job when the election is over."

"Oh yeah? What kind of job?"

"Umm. What about running an MPP's constituency office?"

"We're talking about an MPP from the GTA, not one from North Bay or Goderich?"

"Of course."

"Damn it Jerry!" she says with a huge grin on her face. "You got yourself a communications coordinator."

By the time they return, the dining room has filled up. Volunteers are crowded around the table and those not able to squeeze around the table have spilled over onto sofas and chairs in the adjoining living room. There are coffee cups and bottles of water scattered around the room, on various pieces of furniture. Jerry notices Rick's two sons watching the goings-on from the staircase in the main hall. When Lois goes to answer the front door, the boys disappear up the stairs.

With Rick's agreement, Jerry starts the meeting and thanks everyone for coming out. He introduces himself and lets everyone know that he is Rick's campaign manager. He asks each person to introduce her or himself and indicate what role he or she will have during the campaign. The first to speak is an older woman named Lynette. She has a very stern look and dresses in seventies polyester. She looks like one of those librarians who would be quick to shush you if she caught you talking. She indicates that she is responsible for running the campaign office and managing the volunteers. Jerry adds that she will also keep everyone in line.

Amir is the youngest in the room and looks like a computer nerd - which is exactly what he is. He is tall, thin and wears a bow tie. Amir is the York University grad student recruited by Jerry and is responsible for social media and website development.

After everyone is introduced, Jerry provides some background on the candidate. "I want to introduce you all to Rick Tompkins who is officially the Conservative candidate in BGM. Rick is a personal friend of Peter Lysiak and new to politics. He has strong roots in the community, is a family man and has strong Conservative values. I'm not going to lie to you. This campaign will be an uphill battle, but in recent months, the party has surged ahead in the polls under the leadership of Peter Lysiak. In politics, anything can happen once the writ is dropped. I predict that the election will take place at the end of October, most likely on the twenty-sixth. There will be a lot of work to be done over the next three months. Rick would you like to say a few words?"

"Thank you, Jerry, for that introduction and your optimistic outlook on the election. I just want to thank everyone for coming out this evening. Most of you met my wife Lois when you came in. She is hovering at the entrance right now. We haven't met most of you until tonight. I appreciate that you would give up your time to help me. As Jerry mentioned, I'm new to politics, but I'm ready to kick some butt. Especially Liberal butt."

His comments drew applause from the volunteers. It seems everyone is ready to hit the road running.

———

Ameena 3's family is originally from India and has been living in Mississauga for over twenty years. Although her family still follows many Indian traditions, she is unquestionably culturally assimilated. She lives with her boyfriend, Jacob, in a condo off High Park in West Toronto. Jacob is a hedge fund manager for a mid-sized investment company on Bay Street. They are an odd looking couple. He is tall, blond and stocky. She is short, dark and petite.

She is meeting Jacob for a late dinner at their favorite Thai restaurant in the financial district. When she enters the crowded restaurant she spots Jacob, who has already grabbed a table. She loves how organized her life is since moving in with him. Trips, dinners, the condo: everything is planned out to the tiniest detail. She pushes her way through the crush of people waiting at the front entrance for a table. "Hi Jake. Sorry I'm late but traffic from Brampton was crazy busy." She is shouting to be heard over the noise in the restaurant.

He gets up to give her a hug. "Not a problem. I already ordered drinks. How did the meeting go?"

"Oh god. My friend, Jerry Switzer, is the campaign manager for a loser candidate in Brampton. He asked me to manage the communications."

"What do you mean by loser candidate?"

"Well, for one thing, if you rounded up all the Conservative voters in the riding, you could probably fit them into a Dodge Caravan minivan. There's not much reason to feel optimistic. Then there's the candidate."

He has a puzzled look. "What about the candidate?"

"Well, the best way to describe him is the classic 'square peg in a round hole.' He is socially awkward, politically incorrect and loud. When I met him, the first thing that came to my mind was the school principal from Ferris Bueller's Day Off. Beady eyes, always smirking and a creepy moustache."

The server interrupts to bring them their drinks and take their food order. Jacob decides on pad thai and Ameena 3 orders curry chicken. He returns to their conversation. "So I assume you turned it down?"

"Actually, I accepted."

"Really?" he says with a look of surprise. "Why would you do that?"

"Jerry offered me a pretty good inducement. I will get to run a constituency office for one of the successful candidates and it obviously won't be Rick Tompkins, the guy who is running. It's a great deal for me."

"That's great! I'm really happy for you."

"This is a slam dunk. Like, what could go wrong?" They raise and clink their glasses.

CHAPTER 6

"Our elections are free--it's in the results where eventually we pay." Bill Stern

Jerry knows that summers are a terrible time of the year to try to engage voters. People are focused on vacations, the cottage, backyard BBQs or just about anything that gets them outside. But with Rick's campaign so far behind the other candidates, they can't wait for the fall to get serious about reaching out to voters. Rick is reluctant to put away his golf clubs and Jerry has to literally drag him out to knock on doors.

The other candidates for the upcoming election have been selected and are also out there campaigning. The incumbent is Liberal candidate Sunny Gill, who first won the riding four years ago with forty-seven percent of votes cast. Sunny is an accountant in his mid-forties and has been involved in the Liberal Party and politics since his university days He ran previously for Peel regional council and lost. He has deep roots in the community and provides free financial and accounting advice to members of the community in need. Jerry considers him a lock to be re-elected.

The NDP candidate is Rita Dhillon, a former elementary school teacher who is now selling real estate. Previously, she had been a candidate for the Peel District School Board and the federal Parliament, losing on each occasion. Like Rick, she is really helping her party by running in a riding where there is little chance for victory.

The only other declared candidate is Dana Hiller, who is representing the Green Party. Dana became an environmental activist while working at the Ontario Ministry of the Environment. It is obvious what she will be raising on the campaign trail, but will anyone be listening? These issues are not terribly high on the list of priorities for voters in BGM.

Jerry decides their current priority is to ramp up canvassing. That will require a pool of volunteers to join Rick when he knocks on doors or makes an appearance at community events. He asks Lynette to send out a mass email to potential volunteers and schedules an evening training session at the campaign office. Nine volunteers show up for the session including the two Gore Insurance employees, Ginny and Brittney. The two women concern Jerry. While everyone else is dressed casually in jeans or shorts on a humid August evening, they are anything but casual. Ginny is wearing a short skirt and halter-top with a sequined vest, sneakers and a baseball cap. Brittney has on shorts with a skimpy tank top. She is wearing black open-toed wedge shoes that seem impossible to walk in, though she seems to manage like a veteran tightrope artist making her way across a high wire. Jerry becomes self-conscious that he is staring. Maybe not staring but definitely distracted. The women are very friendly with the other volunteers, perhaps too friendly. One female volunteer is glaring at them with disapproval.

Jerry has the volunteers seated on stacking chairs in a semicircle in front of him. After everyone settles in, Jerry stands up to begin the session.

"Thank you again for volunteering to work with Rick. Canvassing can be a tedious and tiring process. There is one overriding objective behind canvassing: to identify supporters so that on Election Day we can persuade them to come out and vote. This is how it will work. You will be organized into groups to accompany Rick. You will knock on doors. When you find 'a live one', you follow a script that I will provide to determine whether the person will be voting and a possible supporter. Meanwhile, Rick will be on the street. When he sees you chatting with someone, he will join you if he is free to speak to the voter. You will gather data on canvassing forms that I will be providing to you. If no one is home, you leave some campaign literature at the door. The most important thing to determine is how likely they are to vote Conservative."

While speaking, Jerry tries to avoid looking at Brittney's chest but the more he tries to look away the more he feels like a rubbernecker on the highway. "The information collected on the forms will be inputted into a database to be used to identify supporters for Election Day. Does anyone have any questions?"

Ginny raises her hand. "What do we do if we get invited in for a drink?"

Jerry cringes. "Umm, you politely decline. The idea of canvassing is to hit as many doors as possible. Not to make new friends."

Brittney grins. "But there is nothing stopping us from exchanging phone numbers as long as we quickly move to the next door?"

"Sooo...does anyone have a question pertaining to the actual canvassing process?" Jerry answers a few more questions from the group. He is relieved the two Gore employees don't have any other questions. Still, he is experiencing some anxiety over their suitability for this type of work. Maybe it might be more appropriate to have them volunteering in the campaign office. The meeting doesn't last much longer and everyone heads home.

Jerry drops in at Queen's Park to pick up some briefing binders from his office in the Legislative Building. He plans to use the material to prep Rick on issues that might be raised by voters during canvassing. The building is nearly deserted as most politicians and political staff are off somewhere working on the soon to be announced election. It is assumed that the Legislature will not be reconvening in the fall and that means normal business has more or less come to a halt. Jerry takes the stairs up to his office on the third floor. The noise of his shoes on the stone steps echo in the vast stairwell. The building is either stifling hot or freezing cold, never anything in between. Today is a typical summer in the Legislative Building: hot and humid. The unusually empty hallway gives the building an eerie feeling.

He unlocks the door to his office and turns on the lights. His office is stuffy and the dead air makes him wheeze slightly. He quickly grabs some binders off his bookshelf. As he is about to lock up, he hears some sounds in the office next to his. He peers inside and spots Geneva trying to push a box full of reports and papers across the room. As always, Geneva looks like she just walked off of a fashion shoot. She is immaculately dressed, even in jeans. Her long flowing red hair looks perfect and she is wearing red open-toed shoes that match the handbag sitting on her desk. She always wears makeup that looks as if it's been applied by a professional. Jerry suspects this woman has never perspired in her entire life. He knocks on the door. "What brings you to this sweat box on a beautiful summer day and can I give you a hand with that box?"

She looks up at Jerry and then down at her nails. "Oh Switzer, what perfect timing. Could you lift this box and put it on the table over there? I don't want to break a nail."

Jerry grunts as he lifts the box up and slams it down on the table. He leans against the table and turns to Geneva. "What are the latest rumors about an election date? Have you heard anything?"

"All we know is that some time after Labor Day, the Premier will visit the Lieutenant Governor and recommend that she dissolve the Legislature."

"I think everyone knows that much."

"Well If you need to know more, why don't you walk over to Whitney Block and ask the Premier's staff? I'm sure they will be happy to share that information with you."

"You're so snarky. I'm just asking if you heard anything new. I've been hearing the last week of October, which means the twenty-sixth. I'm just trying to plan out a schedule for my candidate."

"Yes, we're hearing the twenty-sixth too. How is the Brampton sacrificial lamb in a tweed jacket, with a moustache that looks like a caterpillar?"

"He's a lazy pain in the ass."

"I suppose you want this election over with already so you can move on. After all, your guy is going down."

"If you must know, I run a professional campaign, win or lose. I am not going to go through the motions."

"Well good luck banging your head against the wall. I've noticed your forehead is beginning to look pretty flat. Our latest polling numbers show your guy running at eleven percent and only a few points ahead of the Greens."

"Oh yeah? What about province-wide? How are we looking?"

"Pretty good. We are showing thirty-four percent, the Liberals are at thirty-seven percent, the NPD are at twenty-two percent and the Green Party is at their usual seven percent. But the undecided voters are at twenty-eight percent. There is lots of room for movement on these numbers."

"Yeah, and two months to win them over."

CHAPTER 7

"The best argument against democracy is a five-minute conversation with the average voter."
Winston Churchill

Jerry uses the briefing binders that he has retrieved from his office to organize some information sessions for Rick. He arranges to meet Rick at his home one evening to review the material. He has chosen topics that are most likely to be raised by voters. Jerry prepares a one-pager for each topic and puts them into a separate binder for Rick.

The first meeting is scheduled late enough in the day to allow Jerry to miss the afternoon rush hour. Rush hour is a misnomer. Traffic is essentially bad all day long in the ring of suburban cities and towns beyond Toronto's borders. It's just that it peaks during the drive to and from work in the morning and afternoon. Despite the fact that traffic is lighter during prime summer vacation time and Jerry tries to avoid the afternoon rush hour, it takes well over an hour to drive to Rick's home. Jerry hates driving and hates going out to the suburbs even more. He considers anything north of highway 401 to be wilderness.

When he finally makes it to Rick's home, he parks his car in a driveway big enough to accommodate an aircraft carrier. Rick answers the door and ushers him into the family room. "Hell, I was hoping you might have forgotten about this. Let's get candidate school over with."

"Nice to see you too, Rick."

"Hey, nothing personal. I'm not big on studying."

Jerry sits down on one of the sofas in the room and pulls out his material. Just then Lois pops her head in the door. "Hello Jerry. Have you had dinner? Can I get you anything?"

"Hi Lois. I've eaten thanks. Maybe just a glass of water."

"Okay, I'll be right back." She disappears into the kitchen and returns with a glass of water and a plate of homemade cookies. Like her mother, Lois always has something baked on hand for company.

Jerry takes a bite out of a cookie. "Wow, these are really good. Thank you, Lois." Jerry turns to Rick and hands him a thin binder. "I have developed one-page notes for the top twenty issues you are likely to hear about from voters. We can also use the notes to prep for any all-candidates meetings that will be organized. These notes reflect the Progressive Conservatives' "Citizens First" platform, which every candidate needs to follow."

Rick nods in agreement. "Who am I to disagree with all the smart people in the party? Do you want to walk me through the issues?"

"That's the plan. Each note spells out the key issue, who is impacted, key messaging and some background info. Let's start with taxes. The party believes taxes are too high and can be lowered by making government more streamlined and efficient. We are promising to lower personal income taxes by ten percent once the deficit is eliminated. A Conservative government would eliminate the budget deficit in four years. We also promise to lower the corporate tax rate to nine percent."

"That sounds simple enough. Do I need to memorize this stuff or will I get to use the notes?"

"You are going to have to learn this stuff. You don't want

to give the appearance that you need to look up the party platform. Please don't make anything up. If you are unsure or can't remember, you advise the voter that the full party platform can be accessed online or we can send them out information."

"Yeah, yeah, what's the next issue?"

Rick's flippant attitude annoys Jerry but he moves on to the next topic. "There is a note on the size of government. We believe the government is bloated and salaries are unrealistic. We are committed to introducing a two-year freeze on salaries of MPPs and public servants. As well, the number of Cabinet Ministers will be reduced by five."

"Seriously, why would we want to freeze our own salaries? That's just dumb."

"It's called spreading the pain around to reduce the cost of government."

"It's still dumb." Rick flips through the binder and stops to read one of the notes. "So let's go over Environment and Energy Policy."

"Conservatives believe that the hydro bureaucracy in Ontario is bloated, which contributes to high hydro rates for consumers. We will get electricity rates under control while investing in nuclear, natural gas and hydroelectric power. Also, we support importing energy from Quebec and other jurisdictions if it will reduce the price for consumers. Any questions?"

"Yeah. Is nuclear power really safe? Look at the accidents that have taken place around the world. I wouldn't want a fucking nuclear plant in Brampton."

"Nuclear power has existed in Ontario for over forty years and no member of the public has ever been harmed as a result of radiation emissions from a nuclear power plant or waste storage facility. In addition, nuclear power has low operating costs and virtually none of the emissions that lead to smog, acid rain or global warming."

"I like the idea of buying nuclear power from other people and letting them deal with the headache of a power plant in their backyard, if you know what I mean." Rick continues to flip through the binder. "Hey, I see a note here about auto insurance. Now that's a topic I know something about."

"Well, the party position is quite simple. The auto insurance system is overly regulated which inhibits innovation and competition. We would eliminate the costly rate approval process and let the competitive marketplace determine price."

"That's it? In Brampton we pay the highest premiums in the country. How would deregulating the rate approval process help the people in this community?"

"Rick, these policies are developed with all voters in mind; they are not specific to any one community. The Conservative Party may not fully address Brampton's auto insurance needs but tax cuts, less bureaucracy and more jobs help everyone. As for auto insurance, deregulation will make rates more competitive everywhere, including Brampton. Insurers are reluctant to lower rates when it takes so much work to reverse a decrease, if their costs go south."

They continue to review notes for another hour at which point Jerry sees that Rick is getting tired. "Let's call it a night. You can try out some of the messaging tomorrow evening at the next canvass."

Rick walks Jerry to the door and they say good night. On the drive home, Jerry feels some relief. The briefing seems to have gone well and Rick seems to have a good grasp of the issues, at least good enough for a one minute chat at a voter's door. Besides, he will be there by Rick's side to provide support.

The canvassers gather in a neighborhood close to Dixie Road for an evening canvass. Besides Rick and Jerry, there are Ginny, Brittney and a volunteer named Luke. Jerry reminds everyone of the process. "The women can work together and Luke, you can go solo today. You knock on doors and just follow the script when talking to voters. What you want to do is determine which way they are leaning. Also if they appear to be a supporter, ask whether they would like to have a lawn sign once the campaign officially begins. Rick and I will be on the sidewalk. If we see that you have someone at the door then we will take over for you, which allows Rick to connect with the voter. If no one answers, leave the literature that I will be handing to you in a moment. Otherwise, hand it directly to the voter. So let's get started."

Jerry decides he needs to stick more closely to Rick who needs more than a short leash; at times, he also needs a muzzle. They notice Luke in a conversation with someone and approach them to join in. Jerry reminds Rick: "Don't worry. I'm going to jump in if you run into any problems."

"Relax buddy, I can handle this just fine." When they reach the door, Rick reaches out to shake hands with the resident. "Hi. I'm Rick Tompkins and I'm the Conservative candidate for the provincial election expected this fall."

The resident is a tall, dark-skinned man with grey hair. He is dressed in a white kurta and churidar, the traditional Indian loose over shirt and tight trousers. He smiles at Rick. "Nice to meet you."

Rick hands him a brochure. "I want you to know that the Progressive Conservatives' "Citizens First" platform will mean more money in your pocket and a smaller government. The highlights are in my campaign literature and online."

"Thank you so much. I will take a look at it."

Rick is eyeballing the man at the door. "Can I ask you

something."

"Yes. What is it?"

"I'm curious. Why do you people wear pajamas all the time?"

"Mr. Tompkins, I'm not wearing pajamas. These are traditional clothing in India, which I happen to find very comfortable."

"But you're in Canada now..."

Jerry instinctively jumps in. "Thank you for your time. We need to move on." He grabs Rick by the arm to lead him back to the street. "You need to avoid insulting people if you want their votes."

"How was that an insult?"

Jerry sighs. "Just stick to the script."

When Rick sticks with the 'approved' messaging, he appears to be a bit of a natural at engaging people. He often slips into the conversation that he happens to be an insurance broker and hands the voters a business card. Jerry pulls him aside and tries to convince him to stick to canvassing but Rick ignores him. The conversation always comes back to insurance and out comes a business card. Jerry begins to understand what is motivating Rick to run. It's good for business. There aren't a lot of 'friendly faces' at the doors. Many voters clearly do not identify with the Conservative Party but they are interested in talking about their insurance premiums.

At the end of the evening, they have knocked on about 300 doors and got about a twenty percent response rate. However, they are only able to identify thirteen voters who are decided on or leaning toward voting Conservative. Jerry finds it a little frustrating. It will be next to impossible to improve on these types of numbers to the point where they might have a chance at winning. The question is how much time they have.

The answer arrives the following morning. His email box

explodes with the news that Premier Lawrence Shedden had met with the Honourable Muriel Patton, Lieutenant Governor of Ontario, who accepted his recommendation that Parliament be dissolved for a general election. The writ for the general election is signed on the next day with the election to take place on October 26th. Now things will get serious, thought Jerry.

CHAPTER 8

"There are worse things in life than death. Have you ever spent an evening with an insurance salesman?"
Woody Allen

The pace of the campaign quickly picks up as Jerry schedules twice daily canvassing for several hours, in the afternoon and evening. Jerry notes that Rick does a good job at connecting with voters but support for a Conservative candidate in the riding is still lukewarm at best. He decides that they should add to their canvassing schedule, greeting commuters each morning at the local GO train stations. The plan is to alternate between the Brampton train station on Church Street and the Bramalea station on Steeles Avenue.

The first train of the day arrives at the Brampton station at 7:01 a.m. and Jerry asks Rick to show up about a half hour before it arrives. On the first morning, Jerry arrives shortly before 6:30 a.m. The parking lot lighting is still on because the sun hasn't quite made it above the horizon. The air is cool and damp from the morning dew, which hangs like fog over the lot waiting to be burned off by the sun.

Jerry pulls out a tote bag with campaign literature from the trunk of his car. There are only a small number of cars in the lot, which will quickly fill up over the next hour. Jerry spots Rick's car pulling into the lot and waves him over. As Rick pulls into the vacant spot next to his car, Jerry notices that Rick has brought Ginny and Brittney — Rick's ever present fan club. Only their inappropriateness exceeds their enthusiasm for canvassing. They appear to have gone to the Miley Cyrus school of fashion. As the women get out of the car, Jerry is quickly annoyed. The two women are both wearing identical black mini shorts (or as the guys at the gym call them: booty shorts), tight 'Vote Rick Tompkins' t-shirts, and black stiletto heels. Jerry wonders how they can tolerate the chilly morning air. The sacrifices these women make for the sake of fashion.

Rick hops out of the car and pumps Jerry's hand. "Good morning Jerry. Don't the girls look incredibly hot?"

"Hot wasn't quite the word I had in mind."

"Look I also thought it would be a good idea to hand out some swag." He removes a large box from his trunk. "I blew the budget on this stuff." He pulls out of the box a red rubber doorstop in the shape of a high heel shoe.

Jerry pulls him aside angrily. "What do you think you're doing? This isn't some tacky trade show. We're running a political campaign here."

"Relax! We need to wake up these sleepy commuters. It's all in fun and will bring some attention to the campaign!"

"I'm not comfortable with this at all. This is all very sexist."

Ginny picks up one of the doorstops. "These are so cool! I've never seen anyone hand out stuff like this during an election. They blow away fridge magnets."

Commuters are beginning to pull into the parking lot and make their way to the train platform. Rick is shaking hands with people as they pass. The two women stand next to him handing out doorstops to puzzled commuters rushing to catch the next train.

"Hey guys! Vote for Rick Tompkins on October 26th!"

Brittney shouts out at two passing men.

One of the men laughs. "I don't even know what party you girls belong to but I'm in!"

Ginny smiles and replies: "Sign up for our email list and you might find out." They both stop to fill out the sign-up sheet. Soon the two women have modified their pitch. "Sign-up and get a chance to win a date." Before long, there is a crowd of men waiting to leave their email address, oblivious to the train pulling into the station.

Jerry stands back and observes the activity, feeling increasingly nervous Usually at commuter canvasses, only an occasional person will stop to chat. People are in too much of a hurry to catch their train. The crowd is different today. Men are clearly hitting on the women who have long since dropped any subtlety and are openly flirting. Some men are taking selfies with the women holding the high-heeled doorstops. Jerry knows he should ask them to tone it down. He turns around and suddenly notices a woman with her arms crossed, glaring at the crowd that has formed. He instantly recognizes Rita Dhillon, the NDP candidate. Jerry approaches to greet her. "Hello Rita, how is the campaigning coming along?"

"You people are disgusting. It really is no wonder that your candidate barely registers above single digits."

"I should explain..."

"In case you didn't know it, the 1950s are over. I guess the exploitation of women is still acceptable in the PC party." Then she marches off to rejoin her people in another corner of the GO station parking lot.

Jerry knows this is going to somehow come back to bite them in the ass before election day. If the campaign headquarters finds out about this, they will be pretty annoyed. Geneva will probably shove one of those doorstops somewhere uncomfortable.

It's just after 8:00 a.m. and the commuters are now scurrying by without stopping. They know if they miss the 8:20 train, there is no other train to follow that day. Jerry sends Brittney and Ginny home and as they say their goodbyes, he pulls Rick aside. "We can't have a repeat of today. The campaign headquarters is not going to be very happy if and when they hear."

"I didn't see anyone complaining."

"Well, it so happens that you missed a visit from Rita Dhillon, who was visibly annoyed."

"Yeah. Why should I care?"

"In case you forgot, there is a candidates' debate in two days. We don't want one of her supporters ambushing you with a question about women's issues."

"Don't you have some kind of note on the topic?"

"No, but now that you mention it, I will have one done and sent to you before the debate. I have a very bad feeling about this."

The sun brightens up the fall sky but Jerry still feels cold and damp. The coffee he brought with him is long gone and his stomach is growling. He pulls out of the parking lot and looks for a place to stop for breakfast to avoid heading into the city at the tail end of rush hour. He comes across a diner just two blocks away from the GO station. The restaurant has an Art Deco look to it, with chrome and green formica tables and a chrome counter with stools. A server directs him to a free table and brings over a pot of coffee to start him off. He sips his coffee while waiting for scrambled eggs and toast and begins to jot down some notes on women's issues for Rick to use. The server brings him his breakfast and, as he is about to eat, his cell phone begins to vibrate. He glances down and sees it's Geneva. "Good morning Geneva. To what do I owe the pleasure?"

"Just checking to see how the star candidate is making out."

"Yeah, I really enjoy a generous serving of sarcasm with my breakfast."

"Oh? Am I keeping you from your bagel? Seriously, Peter asked me to call and see how his buddy is doing?"

"So far, so good. He is doing fine with voters on a one-to-one basis. After all, he sells insurance. But that's part of the problem. He seems to be more interested in finding new insurance clients than attracting voters. A voter will declare they are a Liberal or NDP supporter and instead of moving on, Rick starts talking insurance."

Jerry can feel her frustration over the phone. "Well it's your job to manage him. That's why the job is called campaign manager. You aren't managing the campaign if you aren't managing the candidate."

"This guy can't be managed. Either he's not listening or he doesn't get it. I'm not really sure which one. All I know is this is a riding full of visible minorities and he is saying the most inappropriate things."

"Look, the latest numbers show that we are closing in on majority government territory. The overnight polling shows us at thirty-five percent. We can't have something Archie Bunker says coming back to bite us in the ass."

"Maybe I should tell you about this morning."

"What happened?"

"We did a GO station canvass and Rick showed up with two young women from his office."

"Okay."

"The ladies were wearing outfits more appropriate for clubbing than greeting commuters."

"Shit Jerry! You're supposed to make sure stuff like this doesn't happen."

"Like I said, he's difficult to manage."

"Well, hopefully no one of significance noticed."

"Here's the worst part. The NDP candidate was also canvassing the station and she noticed. We have an all candidates' meeting on Thursday and I wouldn't be surprised if it comes up."

"Okay send me the coordinates for this meeting. I'm showing up."

She hangs up and Jerry turns back to his breakfast. The eggs are cold now and he has lost his appetite. He finishes his coffee and drives back to his place to work on potential damage control for Thursday.

CHAPTER 9

"If opportunity doesn't knock, build a door."
Milton Berle

Jerry cancels all canvassing events for the next two days to concentrate on prepping Rick for Thursday's debate. This is all new to Rick so Jerry sets up a mock debate where he throws out questions and the candidate uses the notes in his briefing binder to respond. At times, Rick has difficulty sticking to the messaging in the notes. The debate sponsor has indicated that the topics to be covered are jobs and the economy, healthcare, education, transit and auto insurance. These are the issues that Jerry spends the most time on with Rick.

The campaign team shows up for the debate about an hour before the start time. The debate is being held in the gym of Brampton Centennial Secondary School and is sponsored by a union local. Jerry doesn't expect it to be a very Conservative-friendly crowd. All the candidates have tables set up just outside the gym, with volunteers handing out literature and chatting with voters. People slowly trickle in and it seems early on that there are more volunteers than actual voters. Ameena 3 is in charge of the Tompkins table and Jerry frequently walks over to check how she and the volunteers are making out.

"Hi Jerry, you look more nervous than the candidate."

"I'm a worrier."

"What's there to worry about? Haven't you prepped Rick enough?"

"I'm always worried. You know that there is always the possibility that our candidate is going to say something inappropriate or off color. Tact is not one of Rick's strengths."

"Yeah, no kidding."

"Ameena 3, how much interest are we drawing tonight?"

"It's been very quiet but the place is full of union members, so no surprise. I've been checking out who is here from the media and it turns out it's not just local media. Kevin Carter is here from the *Star* and Christie Lefebre from the *Sun*."

"There's nothing unusual about that. The Toronto papers make the rounds through the suburbs during an election campaign. It's easier to get a feel for a riding and the candidates by showing up to a debate."

When Rick arrives, he heads over to the Conservative table. He is wearing a dark blue suit, white shirt and blue striped tie. Standard attire for a Progressive Conservative party candidate. He has his binder of notes under his arm. Ameena 3 comes out from behind the table and puts a large Rick Tompkins button on his jacket. "Are you ready to go?"

"As ready as I'm going to be."

"Why don't you stand out here and greet people coming in until it's time to start."

Rick begins to introduce himself and shake hands with people walking in. One tiny elderly Indian woman stops and speaks to Rick in Punjabi. Ameena 3 intercedes and responds to the woman, who smiles and shuffles down the hall. Rick turns to her with a puzzled look in his face. "What was that about?"

"She is looking for the washrooms", Ameena 3 responds with a smirk on her face.

Jerry wanders into the gym, which is slowly filling up. There is a big banner on the north wall declaring "You Are In Buck Country". Next to it are pennants for the 2007 hockey team, the 2008 girls lacrosse team and the 2009 boys basketball team. Also on the north wall is a large photo of NHLer Rick Nash who once attended the school. He notes that there are quite a large number of seniors, which is typical for an all-candidates' meeting. Seniors tend to be some of the most engaged voters and are more likely to have the evening free. He also notices that a significant number of people are wearing union hats. Visible minorities make up nearly half the crowd, which is what one would expect in BGM. Jerry watches Geneva casually stroll into the gym. He waves her over.

"Evening Switzer. Is your guy ready?"

"He's ready."

"You make sure he stays on message."

"Yes, I will remind him. I'll be right back"

Jerry walks out of the gym to avoid having to get into some annoying conversation with her. There are still very few people stopping in front of the Conservative table. He walks over to Rick. "I know I don't need to remind you but Geneva is here and she hasn't driven out to Brampton to provide moral support. You need to keep to the messages in the binder no matter what question is asked."

"Stop worrying, Jerry. Everything is under control."

Several minutes later, one of the organizers politely suggests that people begin to head into the gym so that the debate can begin on time. Jerry wishes Rick good luck and walks back in to sit next to Geneva. In the front of the gym is a long table on a riser with a large name card for each candidate. There is also a name card for the moderator who works for a cable news station in Peel. Next to the table is a lectern. Jerry asks Geneva how the party is doing in some key ridings. She indicates that they are expecting to make big gains in the Ottawa area and the GTA. The Toronto suburbs have really shifted to the Conservative camp. "Even Bramalea-Gore-Malton has seen some improvement. Your guy is drawing close to twenty-five percent which is about even with the NDP candidate, although still twenty points behind the Liberals."

The moderator stands behind the lectern and welcomes the audience. He goes over the format to be followed. Each candidate will be given an opportunity to make opening remarks. The moderator will then ask questions based on the major topics provided to the candidates in advance. That will be followed by questions from the audience. The debate will end with closing remarks from each candidate.

Rick is selected to start off and talks about how the Progressive Conservative Party's priorities are jobs, low taxes, safe communities and less government. There is a small smattering of applause. Sunny Gill, the Liberal candidate is next. He indicates that his party's priority is more money for infrastructure projects, in particular, transit and energy. He speaks briefly in Punjabi. There is a large contingent of Liberal supporters in the crowd who cheer wildly when he finishes. Next to speak is the Green candidate, Dana Hiller. She focuses on environmental issues and transit. Last to go is Rita Dhillon, representing the NDP. She also speaks briefly in Punjabi and focuses her opening remarks on raising corporate taxes and an increase in the minimum wage. She receives significant vocal support from the pro-labor crowd.

The moderator then goes through his list of prepared questions. The candidates run through their party's position on each issue. There is the typical partisan support following each response.

The moderator asks the candidates a question about

funding a light rail transit line in Brampton. When it is Sunny Gill's turn to respond, he looks a little uncomfortable. "The Liberal government recognizes the need to expand our transit infrastructure. To fund future transit, we will impose a small increase in the provincial gasoline tax."

When he is finished answering, the moderator responds. "I'm sorry Mr. Gill but you didn't answer the question. I asked whether a future Liberal government would fund a Brampton light rail line. Would you like to try answering again?"

He shifts uncomfortably in his seat and tries again but basically provides the identical answer. Some members of the audience hiss and boo. Jerry and Geneva smile at the exchange.

Jerry braces himself for questions from the audience. You can prepare for weeks but there will always be that surprise question to make things interesting. In particular when you have a candidate like Rick Tompkins. He can be as unpredictable as the audience. There are a number of local issues raised, some of which are municipal issues rather than provincial ones. Voters often are unable to differentiate which government is answerable for which area of responsibility. An elderly man is recognized by the moderator. He walks to the front of the room. "I don't have a question. I want to make a statement."

The moderator interrupts. "I'm sorry the audience cannot make statements. If you have a question to ask then go ahead. Otherwise, please sit down."

He ignores the moderator. "I'm eighty-two years old and I have something to say. The Canadian Prime Minister is the best prime minister we've ever had. I know because I'm eighty-two."

The Liberal supporters in the room break into applause while everyone else yells for him to sit down. After the moderator restores order, he recognizes a young woman. "I want to ask Mr. Tompkins a question. You have been seen canvassing in the city with two young women who at times might be confused with escorts rather than campaign workers. I would like you to tell me about your attitude toward women."

As Rick grabs the microphone, Geneva glares at Jerry. His chest begins to tighten. "Thank you for that question. The two campaign workers you refer to are enthusiastic volunteers who have dedicated many hours to my campaign. I appreciate their commitment. However, like some women their age, they tend to dress more provocatively than I or some of you may care for. I hope over time they will understand that people may be judging them based on their appearance and how they dress. I have always been respectful towards women. I am pleased that our party has a record number of women running for office on October 26th and I hope that many of them will be successful."

Jerry relaxes a little bit. Rick read the response exactly how Jerry had written it. He looks around and there doesn't seem to be much of a reaction from the audience, although Geneva is still scowling. He feels they may have dodged a bullet on this one. Then near the end of the debate, a middle-aged man gets up to ask a question that turns out to be more of an impassioned plea. "This question is addressed to all the candidates. As you all know, Brampton has the highest auto insurance premiums in the province, maybe in the country. I've heard all of your positions on auto insurance. The Liberals are promising more choice to allow people to buy less coverage. That's not real change. The Conservatives are promising to reduce rate regulation though I have no clue how that would happen. The NDP is promising to improve accident benefits and introduce a consumer's bill of rights for auto insurance. I don't see that lowering my rates. I think the Green Party wants me to give up my car. That's not going to happen either. I've got two cars and two teenage male drivers at home. My premiums are almost equal to my mortgage payments. Is anyone going to do anything to help car owners in Brampton?"

Sunny Gill repeats his government's commitment to introduce more choice to allow consumers to buy down on coverage. That starts some grumbling in the audience and a few hecklers begin expressing their views. When it is Rita Dhillon's turn to respond, she suggests that expanding coverage and reducing rates are both possible. Her response creates some snickering in the room. Jerry can see that Rick is anxious to be handed the microphone. Perhaps too eager. When it's his turn to respond, he rises out of his seat to address the crowd. "My family has worked in insurance for several decades. I'm also a Brampton resident so I know how much it costs to drive in this city. That's why I'm committed to lowering auto insurance premiums by twenty-five percent. For drivers in Brampton, that's a savings of about $700 on average. Some of you might be thinking, how is that possible? The answer is by attacking the source of the problem: lawyers and rehab providers. These two professional groups are exaggerating claims and driving up costs. Drivers are paying more and accident victims are getting less. It's criminal. If I am elected, I will go after these robber barons and make sure your hard earned dollars stay in your pocket."

The room is on its feet clapping and cheering. Rick has found a winning policy position. The problem is it's not one shared by the Ontario Progressive Conservative Party. Jerry turns to Geneva and sees that she is slack-jawed and her face is turning almost the same shade of red as her purse and shoes. She turns to Jerry. "What the fuck is he talking about? You are supposed to be managing him!"

"I told you this guy is next to impossible to manage."

"If there is media in the room, we are in deep shit."

The blood drains from Jerry's face. "Umm, there are reporters here from the *Star* and *Sun* in addition to Mississauga and Brampton media."

"Holy shit!"

Jerry notices that the reporters are rushing to the front of the gym to grab Rick for an interview. He turns to Geneva. "We need to get up there and do some damage control."

When they catch up to Rick, they hear him inform the journalists that more details regarding auto insurance reforms will be coming out in the next few days and that he stands behind his commitment to lower rates by twenty-five percent. Geneva decides that at this point it may be wiser to avoid speaking to the media. She pulls Jerry aside and heads out the door. "We need to talk first thing tomorrow morning. You need to control your trained chimp." With that, she is out the door.

CHAPTER 10

"Those are my principles, and if you don't like them... well, I have others." Groucho Marx

Jerry drags himself out of bed just after 6:00 a.m. half hoping that last night's nightmare was just that, a bad dream. He flips open his laptop and first checks out the online edition of the *Toronto Star*. There it is, as one of the lead news items.

Conservative Candidate Promises
25% Auto Insurance Savings

Kevin Carter, Toronto Star Queen's Park Bureau Chief

A Progressive Conservative candidate running in the October 26th Ontario provincial election has promised to reduce auto insurance premiums by 25%.

Rick Tompkins, a Brampton insurance broker, told an audience on Thursday night in the Toronto suburban riding of Bramalea-Gore-Malton that the Liberal government has done nothing to help drivers in the province. He stated that a Conservative government would lower rates by a quarter. Mr. Tompkins repeated his promise after the candidates' meeting. A Conservative Party spokesperson declined to

---

comment when contacted by the Star. Nowhere on the party's website is there any mention of a promise to lower auto insurance premiums. A spokesperson for the insurance industry was skeptical that rates could be lowered that much. Chip Bonham, vice-president at the Insurance Association of Canada suggested that the Conservatives would have to gut benefits to meet that target.

With just two weeks left until the election, it will be interesting to see what impact this announcement will have on the campaign. Ontario drivers pay much higher premiums than the rest of the country. In Brampton, according to the Insurance Association of Canada, they are the highest of the high, at about $2400 per car, about triple what it costs in Quebec and the Maritimes.

The headline is just as bad in the *Toronto Sun* – *"Tories to lower car insurance rates by 25%."* Jerry feels a large knot forming in his stomach. This is not going to be a stellar day. He notices his phone is buzzing and picks it up. There are thirty-four unread text messages waiting for him. He counts eleven messages just from Geneva. The other messages are from various members in the Conservative campaign team and some media. It's too early to get into it and he hasn't had his coffee yet.

He is about to stumble into the bathroom when his phone begins to ring. "Good morning, Geneva. What a surprise to hear from you at this hour."

"Fuck you, Switzer!"

"Yes, let's just skip the niceties," he sighs, rubbing his eyes with his free hand.

"Your Mr. Tompkins has got a lot of people worked up. There are some people who would like to see him disappear permanently. That being said, there is no early consensus on how to manage this issue. No one was planning to make auto insurance an election issue until the Jason Bourne of politics went rogue and decide to blow a hole through the party platform."

"I was caught completely by surprise as well. He never mentioned to me that he wanted to see insurance rates drop by twenty-five percent. I have no idea where that came from."

"Well, it's out there now. And on the front pages of the papers. There will be a meeting of the campaign team at party headquarters today at 3:00 p.m. and you have been asked to attend. Don't bring Tompkins. I'm sure he is too busy redrafting our positions on nuclear power and taxation."

The line goes dead. Jerry puts down his phone and makes his way to the kitchen to make some coffee. He bought himself one of those single serve coffee makers so that he no longer needs to leave his condo first thing in the morning to enjoy a coffee while going over the news. He likes it that he doesn't need to get dressed to get his fix of caffeine. However, no amount of coffee is going to prepare him for today. He checks his laptop to see if anyone else has picked up the story. Nothing so far but it's early. He decides to jump into the shower before his day spins out of control. While drying off he picks up his phone and sees there are two phone messages. They are both from reporters, one from Global News and the other from CTV, looking for interviews. He decides it's best not to return the calls for now.

He suddenly realizes that he'd better make sure no one else on the team speaks to anyone in the media until the party decides on some damage control messaging. He first calls Rick.

"Good morning Rick. Have you seen the headlines?'

"Morning Jerry. Yeah and I like them."

"Well unfortunately, I doubt Peter does or anyone else on the campaign team for that matter."

"Yeah, I guess I didn't quite follow the party line. But it's what I believe."

"This is politics. No one really cares what you believe. In fact you need to keep your beliefs to yourself. Now there are going to be reporters who will want to interview you if they haven't already tried to reach you. Do not speak to anyone until I get back to you later today. It's best to stay low right now."

"Wow, is this that serious?"

"It is. I'll talk to you later." Next he dials Ameena 3 who picks up on the first ring.

"Hey Jerry. I saw the headlines. What's happening? People must be freaking out."

"You know it. First, has anyone in the media contacted you?"

"I just got a call from someone from CanIndia News but I haven't called back yet."

"Good. Don't speak to anyone. I've got a meeting at campaign headquarters this afternoon. I'll get back to you with some messaging cooked up by the spin guys. I've spoken to Rick but make sure everyone else knows too."

"Will do. Good luck today."

"Thanks."

Jerry spends the rest of the morning scanning the online news and social media. The Canadian Press picks up the story by mid-morning, which means it will be in every newspaper in the province by tomorrow. Just after lunch, he decides to walk to the campaign office on Adelaide Street. He always prefers to walk, even in bad weather. It's one of those miserable grey fall days. There's a light rain falling. At times, the wind drives the rain sideways and strains the frame of Jerry's umbrella. After a few blocks he is so wet that he concedes to the weather gods and ducks into the subway. His bad luck continues. A crackly voice on the TTC public address system announces that there is an ill patron on the track level (also known as a jumper) at Bloor station. Not that he can make out what the crackly voice is saying. He has to ask a TTC employee for an interpretation. About twenty minutes later, subway service is restored and Jerry finds himself crammed into a subway car with a knapsack digging into his ribs and a shoulder continually hitting his head. If he was a farm animal, there would be animal rights protests in front of the TTC headquarters.

He is still early for the meeting when he finally emerges from the subway system so he decides to stop at a Starbucks for a double espresso. He begins to work through in his head how the campaign team might deal with this dilemma. Up to this point, the Conservative campaign has been error-free. They could decide to just drop Rick as a candidate. After all, it's not like he has a chance of winning the riding. Cutting him loose will make it easier for the party to distance itself from his comments. He pulls out his phone and notices that the CTV reporter has called again and now a *Globe and Mail* reporter has also left a message. He gets up and walks down the block to the building housing the party headquarters. The offices are on the fourth floor and while Jerry waits for an elevator, Geneva arrives. Other than "hello," they barely acknowledge each other on the ride up. She is obviously in a foul mood so he avoids initiating a conversation.

Jerry follows her into a large boardroom with a long, dark wood table surrounded by wide, black chairs with plush cushioning. Looking out the rain-streaked windows, everything looks wet and grey out. He grabs a vacant seat near the middle of the table. People begin to appear and find a place to sit. Jerry recognizes the attendees although he hasn't met them all before. In addition to Jerry, Geneva, and Peter Lysiak, there are the campaign co-chairs, Donna Brown and Cam Pulver; a pair of policy advisors, Karim Reza and Leslie Geko; and the campaign communications director, Lina Nesterov. Cam is chairing the meeting and brings everyone to order.

"Thank you everyone for making yourself available on such short notice. As you all know by now, our candidate in Bramalea-Gore-Malton, Rick Tompkins, set off a bomb for us last night with a promise to reduce auto insurance rates by twenty-five percent. Not exactly a modest commitment. Lina, can you give us a summary of media reaction?"

"Both the *Star* and *Sun* had reporters at last night's debate and published stories this morning. The *Star's* article is on the front page. There is also print coverage in a couple of Peel papers. The CP picked it up this morning. We have had over a dozen media requests for comment. I've been telling them that we will get back to them."

Peter jumps in. "So what are our options?"

Geneva is quick to respond. "I think the only way to walk away from this mess is to have him step down as a Conservative candidate."

Peter has a pained look on his face. "I don't know. I'm not comfortable with that. It's not because Rick is a friend of mine. We have candidates who on occasion misspeak or over promise. This might not be a riding we can win but the next one might be. Isn't it possible that this is a one-day blow up that will be forgotten by tomorrow?"

Donna jumps in. "Peter, car insurance has been a contentious issue in past elections and not just in Ontario. The issue just about tripped up the New Brunswick PC party under Bernard Lord in 2003."

Cam turns to Karim. "How feasible is Tompkins' suggestion? Have we heard from the insurance industry?"

"I spoke to an official at the Insurance Association of

Canada and he is suggesting that a twenty-five percent premium reduction is impossible without introducing a totally different insurance system. He is very pessimistic."

Cam has a smirk on his face. "I would be shocked if he would have said anything different. Those insurance people make billions being pessimistic. As I see it, we have several possible options. We can get the candidate to clarify that he may have overstated possible savings and that it is something south of twenty-five percent. We would still have to come up with a number. Another option is to get him to continue to talk about auto insurance reforms but distance ourselves from his views. Turn him into a maverick of sorts. We could use him to undermine the Liberals on this issue. However, we might be undermining our own weak position at the same time. Finally, we could just adopt the twenty-five percent rate reduction as one of our long-term goals on this file. Are there any other options?"

Jerry jumps in. "I am thinking we could promise if elected to establish a formal review process to identify changes that would reduce auto insurance rates in the province. I know it's not going to excite voters like a promised rate reduction but this twenty-five percent figure could come back to bite us in the ass."

Donna shakes her head. "A review? That's something the Liberals would do. I don't like it."

Cam raises an additional concern. "It looks like a cynical piece of backtracking."

Leslie, who has been quiet up until now, gets everyone's attention. "I just picked up some interesting polling data you might want to consider. Voter support for the PCs is up four percent overnight with Liberals dropping by three percent and the NDP dropping by one percent. If you think the new polling numbers have nothing to do with yesterday, then listen to this. When voters were asked which issues were most important to them, last week nineteen percent indicated auto insurance premiums. Since last night that number has gone up to forty-four percent. I'm not done. Your Rick Tompkins was running third in the BGM riding last week with less than twenty-five percent of support. Today, he is dead-even with the Liberal candidate at thirty-six percent."

Peter looks around the table. "It seems a twenty-five percent rate reduction resonates with voters. Maybe we should grab this issue before someone beats us to it. Everyone has access to the same polling data. Besides, I think all the other options lack any conviction." Heads around the table nod in agreement.

Jerry looks over to Geneva, who looks rather agitated. She jumps in. "I can't believe what I'm hearing. This guy was only supposed to put up some campaign signs so that people in the riding would know we had a candidate running. Now he's driving policy for us? I wouldn't trust him to drive the campaign bus. Come on people, this is nuts!"

Peter shakes his head. "That was before yesterday. I acknowledge that we intended to avoid talking about auto insurance during the campaign. But the 'genie is out of the bottle', as they say. This issue is not likely going to go away." Geneva slumps back into her chair.

Lina makes the following suggestion. "Peter, I'm with you on this. I would suggest that you to hold a press conference first thing tomorrow morning. You can appear with Rick Tompkins to state that the PC party agrees with Rick and supports a twenty-five percent reduction in auto insurance premiums. You will promise that details on how that will be achieved will come out following a Conservative victory on October 26th."

Cam makes one additional suggestion. "We need to call the Insurance Association of Canada and give them a heads up. They will hate what we are doing but will not likely rock the boat.

Tell them we will work with them on reforms after the elections. Unless someone has something to add, let's close the meeting and get a presser set up for the morning."

Jerry walks out of the meeting in a state of shock. Rick makes a promise based on no research, no consultations, nothing at all. Now the party is throwing out their campaign strategy to run with his stupid idea. To him, this feels like a house of cards. Hopefully, it won't collapse in the next two weeks.

CHAPTER 11

"Were it left to me to decide whether we should have a government without newspapers or newspapers without a government, I should not hesitate for a moment to prefer the latter."
Thomas Jefferson

The Insurance Association of Canada's offices are located in an older, unattractive downtown office building, just a five-minute walk from the Ontario Legislative Building. The trade association has traditionally been underfunded by its members who constantly complain that their companies are not profitable. After the Conservative campaign team meeting to discuss the Tompkins affair, the Ontario Committee of the trade association calls a meeting to discuss the upcoming Conservative Party announcement on auto insurance. The twelfth floor boardroom is dominated by an old mahogany table that is badly in need of refinishing. Jugs of water are placed around the table by staff because the Association does not believe in paying for bottled water. The table is surrounded by black naugahyde chairs. The room hasn't changed much in almost forty years. At the table are the presidents of the eleven largest insurance companies in the province and Chip Bonham, the Ontario VP at the Insurance Association of Canada. Chip provides the committee members an update on the latest campaign developments.

"The announcement by Mr. Tompkins in Brampton caught us all by surprise. A rate reduction was never part of the Conservative platform. I spoke to a senior campaign official to find out why we weren't given a heads up. The story I got was that this guy blindsided the party."

John Leifer, one of the younger CEOs, responds. He is a gregarious American and the only person in the room that hasn't gone grey. "Chip, I think they are feeding you a lot of BS. I bet this was planned all along but they didn't want the industry to know. We should consider pulling our support for the party."

"Hang on there, John. The Conservatives are totally supportive of the industry. We've spent the past two years helping them understand our business and develop their position on auto insurance. If this was something they were thinking about, we would have known."

Dan Little, president of Prima Insurance, the largest company in Canada, jumps in. "Fine, we didn't know about it. But we do now. I hope the IAC plans on sending out a press release slamming this ridiculous promise. This is just shameless pandering to voters."

Chip has a pained look. "Actually, I've been invited to a press conference tomorrow morning in Brampton to support the rate reduction announcement. It seems the Conservatives have decided to adopt this position because it makes for good politics."

The room explodes. A furious John Leifer shouts out. "They can go to hell! There is no way the IAC is going to be anywhere near that press conference."

Chip tries to take back control of the meeting. "Settle down everyone. Let's not overreact. Let's remember that Peter Lysiak and his party are very pro business. This is a lot of campaign rhetoric and if it helps get them elected, that's good for us. After the election, we sit down and explain to them how unattainable their promises are. Over time, we will work on getting them to move off this position."

Kathy Beech, the only female in the room, responds. "I'm not comfortable with any of this but I know wacky things happen during elections. Chip, you have my support. I don't see a problem with holding back public criticism on something that is obviously very popular on the street. But we shouldn't be seen as endorsing it, either. And that doesn't prevent us from expressing our opposition in private." A number of heads nod in agreement.

Chip gazes around the room. "Good. I will make an appearance at their 'dog and pony show' tomorrow. Publicly, we will be silent on the rate reduction promise other than to say we are awaiting details of their plan before commenting. In the meantime, I will have IAC staff draft a letter that properly reflects the industry's perspective on such an absurd promise. A draft will be circulated to committee members tomorrow."

━━━━━━━

The following morning, a press conference is organized in the lobby of Brampton City Hall at Wellington and Main. An unwinnable riding in Brampton has become ground zero for the PC party election campaign. Jerry arrives with Rick and Ameena 3. Rick has been told he will stand on the podium next to Peter along with a reluctant Chip Bonham.

It's about thirty minutes before the press conference is scheduled to begin and the media representatives are already staking out a spot in front of a podium that has been set up on a riser. Out on the street, there are already a number of vehicles from the major news stations unloading equipment. Ameena 3 begins chatting with some reporters to pick up some intelligence while Jerry pulls Rick aside to keep him away from any eager reporters looking for an impromptu quote.

"This is Peter's show and you are just here for support. Peter will make his announcement and then he will open it up for a few questions. Also, last night I sent you an updated note on our position on auto insurance premiums."

Rick responds with a smirk. "I saw that. It looked vaguely familiar."

"This is just an FYI. You aren't to speak. If someone asks you a question, you are to defer it to Peter."

"I hear ya."

Ameena 3 drifts over to join in the conversation. "The buzz from the 'media hacks' is that this announcement could be a game changer. However, they will not be giving us a free pass. The more cynical ones see this sudden change in direction as a way to cover for a blunder by Rick. They plan to grill Peter on it."

Rick sneered. "What a bunch of scum bags!"

Jerry is about to respond when he notices Peter Lysiak and his entourage enter the lobby. Accompanying him is Chip Bonham. Jerry directs his group over to the podium to meet them. Lina Nesterov addresses the staff. "We are on a tight schedule so let's get started. Chip, you will stand to Peter's right and Rick, you're on the left."

They take their positions behind the podium. Jerry moves to the back of the scrum with Ameena 3. Between them and the podium are over twenty reporters with their cameras, lights and microphones. Some reporters are using their smartphones to record the press conference.

Lina steps up to address the collection of scribes and pundits. "Good morning everyone. Let's get this presser underway. I'm Lina Nesterov, director of communications for the Ontario

Progressive Conservative Party's election campaign. Conservative Leader Peter Lysiak has an important campaign announcement to make this morning. Joining him is Rick Tompkins, who is the Conservative candidate in Bramalea-Gore-Malton, and Chip Bonham with the Insurance Association of Canada. Mr. Lysiak will read a statement and then we will open it up for questions."

Peter steps forward and begins his statement. "High car insurance premiums have plagued Ontarians for far too long. Ontario drivers pay more for car insurance than drivers in every other province. As my friend and colleague Rick Tompkins points out, no one pays more than the hard working citizens of Brampton. The Liberal government has tinkered with the system to create an illusion that they are managing it. The truth is the system suffers from neglect. The Progressive Conservative party is prepared to make significant changes to bring down premiums. We will reduce rates by twenty-five percent within two years of forming a government. That's an average annual savings of $375 for drivers in the province. For communities like Brampton, where premiums are much higher, the potential savings are much more. Although we have always believed that we need a more efficient and cost effective system, our party has never set any premium reduction targets. We are prepared to do that today. Standing to my right is Chip Bonham representing the insurance industry. Chip is here because the insurance companies would also like to see drivers, their customers, save money. We don't have the details as of yet but this will be one of our priorities following the election. I will take a few questions."

"Elsie Brenner, Global News. Why this sudden change in policy direction with just two weeks left in the campaign? This appears to be a knee jerk reaction and not very well thought out."

"We have always supported lower rates for drivers. Now we

are ready to commit to a specific and real target. Rates will go down by twenty-five percent within two years."

"Kevin Carter, *Toronto Star*. I attended the candidates' meeting the other night when Mr. Tompkins made his off the cuff remarks and now they are part of your party's platform. Isn't this a case of the tail wagging the dog?"

"The Liberal government has continued to burden drivers with high insurance rates just as they have burdened taxpayers with high taxes. This is another important pocketbook issue that we plan to champion. A Conservative government will save drivers an average of $375 a year on their premiums."

"Greg Slavens, CityNews. Are you prepared to release details of how you plan to lower premiums? Don't drivers have a right to know how you plan to achieve such dramatic rate savings?"

"Yes they do. The details will be provided after we have had discussions with the insurance industry and other key stakeholders, following the election. Any changes that we plan to introduce will favor consumers." Peter turns to Rick. "Rick, you work in the insurance sector. Do you have anything to add to that?"

Jerry and Ameena 3 glance at each other nervously. This was not part of the plan.

"I sense that some of you are skeptical. How can we possibly bring down rates this much? The truth is that no one has ever had the nerve to go after the source of the problem: lawyers and rehab providers. Exaggerated claims are driving up costs. In the end, drivers are paying more."

Jerry winces. Now the party appears to be ready to go to war with lawyers and health care workers. What happened to the "Citizens First" platform? What about taxes and the economy? The party is so close to taking this election, so why risk it all with this buffoon? What does he know about election campaigns?

"Christie Lefebre, *Toronto Sun*. I have a question for Rick Tompkins. We hear there are sexist elements to your campaign, namely two young women who appear to be more than just campaign volunteers. Can you provide any clarification on these women and their role in your campaign?"

Jerry senses panic setting in. He leans over and whispers to Ameena 3. "The press conference may be spinning out of control."

"The two campaign workers you refer to are employees at my brokerage firm. They have dedicated many hours to my campaign and I appreciate their commitment. Their role is no different than any other volunteer working on my campaign. I should add that the Conservative Party has a record number of women running for office on October 26th and I hope that many of them will be successful." Jerry and Ameena 3 look at each other with their mouths wide-open. Their candidate nailed that answer.

After several more questions, Lina gets up again. "This ends the formal part of our announcement this morning. Thank you again for coming out. Peter will be available for a few more minutes and then we must move on to our next campaign event."

Later that day, the Liberals respond to the Conservative announcement with their own announcement. The Liberals plan to appoint Clifford Lewis, an economics professor at the Schulich School of Business, and Doreen Muir, a law professor at Osgoode Hall Law School, to lead an auto insurance review with a mandate to bring down the cost of insurance in the province while improving consumer protection.

The tail is now in complete control of the dog.

CHAPTER 12

"A man without money needs no more fear a crowd of lawyers than a crowd of pickpockets." R. Rinkle

It's still dark. Jerry rolls over to pick up his smartphone, which is buzzing on his bedside table. Through the fog of sleep, he can make out that it is Geneva. "What time is it?"

"Switzer, why is it that you're always sleeping when I call?"

"That's no coincidence. You fucking call at night. People on the other side of the world might be up. Why don't you call someone in New Zealand and let me sleep." He notices it's 5:45 a.m., just about time to get up anyway. "So what's up?"

"Well, I don't know if I want to tell you anymore, after getting such a warm greeting."

"Good, then I'll go back to sleep."

"I have in my hands the latest polling data but you don't sound terribly interested so I'll let get back to sleep."

"I'm awake! Let's hear what you've got."

"We got a nice bump from the insurance announcement the other day. We are polling at forty percent, which not only translates into a win if the numbers hold until Election Day but we are close to majority territory. The Liberals have dropped to thirty-three percent, the NDP have dropped to twenty percent and the Greens are holding at seven percent."

"That's incredible!"

"Switzer, you're going to get all warm and fuzzy when I give you the numbers for BGM. Captain Twenty-Five Percent has the lead with forty-two percent. The Liberal incumbent has dropped to thirty-one percent. That NDP candidate, who has been harassing your guy, has dropped to twenty-two percent. Even the Green candidate lost support and is at five percent."

"I'm stunned. And you wanted to dump Rick and the rate reduction proposal. The PC candidate only picked up seventeen percent in the last election. I really need to concentrate on getting the vote out now."

"Well, there is always the potential for a screw up so let's not start doing a victory lap quite yet. The other reason I am calling is that we have been getting a lot of noise from the Committee for Fair Auto Insurance. They are a group of personal injury lawyers."

"I've never heard of them."

"They aren't particularly active until a politician mentions auto insurance reforms and then suddenly they appear. They exist only to protect their turf, which happens to be the forty percent they take off the top of every insurance settlement and court award. We are meeting with their executive and Peter would like Captain Twenty-Five Percent to be there. Since you are his handler, you need to be there too. The meeting is scheduled for tomorrow morning at 10 a.m. at the offices of Blidswell Morgan."

Jerry hears the line go dead. This is just another interrupted sleep, which he realizes is going to continue to happen a lot with just eight days remaining until the election. Before heading for the shower, he first checks for phone messages. One message that catches his attention indicates that the Ontario Rehabilitation Council along with the Ontario Auto Accident Victims Alliance have scheduled a joint press conference this morning to denounce possible auto insurance benefit cuts by the Conservatives. The opponents are mobilizing quickly. He knows that their voices will largely fall on deaf ears when his party is offering twenty-five percent premium reductions. He sends a text message to Ameena 3 asking her to head over to the press conference.

After breakfast he drives to Brampton to meet with Lynette, at the campaign office. They briefly discuss the process for getting the vote out on Election Day. There is no point in spending weeks reaching out to supporters and then having them sit at home on the day of the election. The problem in this riding is that there has been a late shift to the Conservative camp. That means the data they've collecting while canvassing is largely out-of-date. Their data shows a small number of Conservative voters but recent polls show the numbers have grown. Lynette is a veteran of many election campaigns so Jerry leaves this in her capable hands.

Next Jerry meets up with Rick and some volunteers for another long day of canvassing. Rick has become enthusiastic about canvassing. Earlier in the campaign, he was met with a scowl at many doors in this Conservative wasteland. Suddenly, he is a celebrity candidate and greeted with friendly handshakes. Some people ask if they can have a 'selfie' taken with him. He is no longer asking voters if they would like one of his business cards because they are asking on their own. In this riding, auto insurance has become the only issue on the minds of voters.

Ameena 3 reports back from the press conference. She indicates that the media turnout was small. The reporters are waiting to see the details on how rates will come down. Until then, there is nothing to critique. Strangely, no one seems to be questioning whether a twenty-five percent reduction is actually possible. The press conference does generate some headlines for one day for those who may have noticed page eight of their newspaper or minute twelve of the local television news broadcast.

———

In the morning, Rick and Jerry travel together by cab into Toronto's financial district for the meeting with the Committee for Fair Auto Insurance. The offices of Blidswell Morgan are located on the thirty-first floor of the Bay Adelaide Centre. When they reach the firm's reception area, they are ushered into a 600-square foot boardroom with a spectacular view of the city facing south, overlooking Lake Ontario. The lake is slate grey this morning, caused by the heavy cloud cover. The wind has churned up the water, creating tiny white caps. Jerry follows the path of a small Porter Airlines Dash 8 approaching the landing strip on the Toronto Island airport. As the room fills up, he turns to the others. Already seated are Peter and Geneva as well as a number of youngish lawyers in expensive black suits, twiddling away on their iPhones. Jerry can't help but notice the tight black skirt that Geneva is wearing that ends well above her knees. He decides it's a good effort on her part. Distract the chauvinist hoard with some legs. A few more lawyers arrive as does Cam Pulver, representing the campaign team.

After introductions are made, one of the lawyers leads off the discussion. "I'm Graham Wallace, a partner at Blidswell Morgan and your host for this meeting. Peter, our group would like to thank you and your team for meeting with us just days before the election. We know how busy you must be and appreciate you making time for us. We have followed your announcement on auto insurance with great interest. Like other voters, we are interested in your plan to reduce rates for drivers by twenty-five percent. This seems to have come out of nowhere. We are also aware that at a recent public meeting, Mr. Tompkins referred to lawyers as robber barons. Naturally, we are concerned that lawyers are being made out to be villains in an effort to garner votes. We find the practice objectionable. Lawyers play an important role in the system by advocating for accident victims, facilitating access to rehabilitation and reaching settlements for clients so that they can go on with their lives."

Peter tries to reassure the group. "Thank you for your frankness, Graham. We have no details as of yet on how to reduce rates but we believe it to be achievable. We also believe that the Liberal government is mismanaging this file, which badly needs some firm and attentive stewardship. Now I'm sure you are aware that during the heat of a campaign, there can be some inflammatory language used. You shouldn't be worried about it. We have a great amount of respect for the plaintiff bar and look forward to working with you once we form the next government. Rick, do you have anything to add to that?"

Before Rick begins to speak, Jerry is already cringing. Rick without a script is like juggling live grenades. It's only a matter of time before something blows up.

Rick stares angrily across the room "I guess it's up to me to play the bad cop here. I know you guys skim forty percent off of every insurance settlement. Well, I'm the guy who is going to hold the line." With that he slams his fist on the dark oak table. "You and all the other leeches have sucked enough out of the system."

Geneva jumps right in. "Rick is just repeating campaign rhetoric but we look forward to working with you after the election. Isn't that right, Rick?"

Wallace brusquely responds. "This is an interesting way to develop a working relationship."

Rick is now on his feet. "You know how you can tell a lawyer is lying? His lips are moving!"

The meeting quickly deteriorates. Geneva glares at Jerry and appears to mouth the words 'I'm going to kill you.' One lawyer shouts out over the ruckus. "If you people form the next government, it's going to be a disaster!"

Peter tries to calm the situation. "People! Let's discuss this in a civilized manner." He is ignored.

One lawyer is jabbing his finger in the air in the direction of Rick. At one point, it appears as if Rick might grab that finger and snap it off. Rick glares at him. "Get your goddamn finger out of my face!" Then to add to the drama, Rick gets up and shouts out, "I've had enough of you ambulance chasers," and storms out of the room with Jerry chasing after him. As they ride down in the elevator, Rick turns to Jerry with a big smile on his face. "Wasn't that a great performance? Let's get some beer."

CHAPTER 13

"A vote is like a rifle: its usefulness depends upon the character of the user." Theodore Roosevelt

The volunteers show up at the Tompkins campaign office at 8:00 a.m. on Election Day. Lynette provides last minute instructions and each person is given an area within the riding for which they will be responsible. Each is handed a package that they will use the rest of the day to monitor Conservative supporters who have yet to vote. Everyone is feeling confident that Rick will win, but actually getting the vote out is still necessary.

Jerry had voted in an advance poll and heads directly to the campaign office to assist with election day activity. The long days leading up to Election Day have left him exhausted. However, the excitement about what is certain to be a victory is keeping him energized through the day. Should the Progressive Conservatives win the election as expected, Jerry is confident that his next position will be a key job in the Premier's office. Working next to the seat of power would be a dream come true for a policy wonk. The last polls released before the election indicate a possible Conservative majority but Jerry knows that pollsters have been known to be wrong.

Rick votes first thing in the morning and then heads to the office. At this point, there is nothing he can do other than wait for the results. He decides it's best to immerse himself in his work until the polls close. He has that 'butterflies in the stomach' feeling all day long and finds it almost impossible to concentrate on the simplest tasks. The days goes by so slowly but finally the work day ends and Rick heads home for dinner. The plan is to watch the results at home with Lois and then join a campaign celebration with the volunteers at a local restaurant, later in the evening.

When the polls close at 9:00 p.m., Jerry is still in the campaign office waiting for volunteers to phone in results for each polling station in the riding. He keeps a close eye on the TV for election results. Early returns show the Conservatives taking an early lead. When the Legislature was dissolved, the Liberals held fifty-eight seats, with the NDP as the official opposition holding twenty-eight seats. Within forty-five minutes, all the networks are predicting the Progressive Conservatives will win a majority. Normally reserved, Jerry lets out a scream on hearing the news. By the end of the evening, their final count is sixty-one seats and forty-one percent of votes cast. The Liberals are relegated to official opposition and the NDP are dropped to third party status.

Rick and Lois have an anxious evening at home. They say very little as they watch the results. Over the course of the campaign, something has changed in Rick. At the start, he was only looking at helping out Peter and finding some new insurance clients. Then a combination of an election issue he cared about and his competitive nature took over. In the final two weeks of the campaign, he actually wanted to win. He wanted to win badly. He is now a bundle of nerves, watching the election coverage. It turns out that the race in Bramalea-Gore-Malton is a nail-biter. He and Liberal Sunny Gill are neck and neck throughout much of the evening Around 10:45 p.m., Rick is finally declared the winner with thirty-eight percent of votes, a much lower number than suggested by polls. Sunny Gill does a great job getting Liberal supporters to the polls but falls short with just over thirty-six percent of votes.

Rick and Lois head to the campaign party, which has become quite loud and spirited with the news of the results. As Rick's campaign gained momentum, it also picked up many new volunteers. As a result, the restaurant is packed when Rick and Lois walk in. Rick is beaming as one person after another comes to shake his hand or slap him on the back. Jerry makes his way over to give both Rick and Lois a big hug. He leans over to Rick so he can be heard. "I'm stunned. We actually did it!"

"Jerry, I couldn't have done this without you."

"It was a team effort. All these people had a hand in the results. Which is why you need to say a few words to thank all your volunteers." Rick nods in agreement.

Ameena 3, who is right behind Jerry, pops up onto a chair and yells out to the crowd. "I have just confirmed with Elections Ontario that the next Member of the Provincial Parliament representing Bramalea-Gore-Malton is Rick Tompkins!" The restaurant breaks out in wild cheering. The volunteers begin chanting "We want Rick! We want Rick!"

Rick steps forward and waves to the crowd which continues to chant. It eventually quiets down enough for Rick to make a few remarks. "What a great day it is to be a Progressive Conservative." Rick pauses as the room explodes once again. "Voters in Ontario have rejected a government that constantly has a hand in the taxpayers' pockets and have supported a party that puts citizens first. I can tell you, I'm going to Queen's Park to kick some ass. Those spineless bureaucrats will have Rick Tompkins to deal with now." Everyone is up clapping and stomping their feet.

"I want to thank a few people who made this possible. I

had some great people on my team: Jerry, Ameena 3 and Lynette. Then all of you wonderful people who knocked on doors, stood in cold, wet GO station parking lots, and drove around putting up signs. I wouldn't be here without you. Special thanks to my wonderful wife Lois who has stood by me for twenty years. I never expected to win. Now, here I am. I'm ready to fight for the people of Brampton and to keep the government out of your pockets and deliver lower auto insurance rates!" Rick pumps a fist in the air and the room goes absolutely crazy.

Jerry is chatting with Lois while watching a crowd of people waiting in line to shake Rick's hand. "He will never be at home. You see that line of people? There will be a similar line outside his office all the time."

"I'm ready for what comes next."

"So how do you feel about this? Political wives either remain in the background away from the limelight or use their status to further their own ambitions."

"I'm happy for Rick. Despite his limitations, which I'm well aware of, I think he is a capable guy. I told him upfront that he could win. Now it's up to him to grow into his new role. As for me, I'm an old-fashioned gal. I just want to make sure we maintain a stable family life."

"Well, I'm sure you will keep things on an even keel at home."

"So what will you do, Jerry?"

"I expect to be given a job within the government. I'm hoping it will be in the Premier's office. That would be my dream job. As you probably know, I worked in Peter's office before the election."

"I hope that works out for you. We both appreciate how hard you've worked these past few months. Rick told me that Peter called earlier in the evening to congratulate him and to thank him for helping the party. He mentioned to Rick that he has plans for him."

"That's great. Maybe he'll be appointed a parliamentary assistant."

"What do they do?"

"They help ministers with some important files and, although not members of the cabinet, sit on some important committees."

"That would be really nice for Rick."

Jerry notices his phone vibrating and pulls it out of his pocket. "Hi Mom." He moves to a corner of the restaurant so he can hear better.

"We haven't heard from you in so long. I wanted to make sure you were still alive before filing a missing person report with the police."

"Yes, I'm still alive and well. I've just been busy."

"Did you hear the Conservatives won the election?"

"Yes Mom, I heard."

"How did that Tom person make out?"

"Tom who?"

"You know, the fellow you've been helping."

"His name is Rick, Rick Tompkins," he says with a sigh. "He won as well."

"Your Uncle Arthur says the Conservatives will ruin the province. He is such a socialist. Your father calls him a communist."

"Mom, this isn't a great time to talk. How about I drop by for dinner on Friday?"

"Oh my! My very important son is going to find an hour for his elderly parents. I'll have to get out the good china."

Jerry ignores the sarcasm. "I'll see you on Friday. Bye." Before putting away his phone, he checks his messages. There is one from Geneva.

Congratulations on winning George Castanza a seat in the Legislature! lol

Very funny.

What an incredible night. Did you see Peter's victory speech? Yes. Very moving.

Want to join me for a celebratory drink?

Seriously?

I'm sitting at the bar in Sherlock's on King Street all alone. :(

Why are you in a bar alone?

I left the campaign party. It was too noisy. I'm in the mood for some quiet celebrating.

Ah yes, the reflective Geneva takes over tonight.

So are you coming?

Are you sure you want me to join you?

That's why I'm texting you. Hey we can catch up.

We've both been so busy.

Okay. I can be there in 30 minutes.

Jerry returns to Lois and says good night. He hops into his car and makes his way downtown. He knows it's odd that Geneva would duck out from the campaign celebration but he also understands that the woman is an introvert. But why invite him? At work, their relationship has been frosty at times. Though, when they've met for drinks or dinner, she really has been a different person. It's going on midnight, so there isn't much traffic on the roads although the Entertainment District is never quiet at this hour. There is plenty of traffic for Jerry to contend with but he eventually finds a parking lot and heads over to Sherlock's. He immediately spots Geneva sitting at the bar flirting with one of the bartenders. She is wearing a pair of stretch denim jeans that look like they were painted onto her legs. She is wearing a blue crop top and, to his surprise, her navel is pierced. When she spots him, she gives him a high five. "Switzer, pull up a seat and join me for some vodka shots."

Jerry looks at her. She is loud and obviously drunk. "How many of these have you had?"

"Who's counting? Have you met Nick the bartender? Nick, pour my colleague and me some vodka." Nick pours them each a shot of vodka, which they throw back. "So your dumbass insurance salesman with the geeky moustache is an MPP." She is laughing at the thought. "How fucked up is this world?"

"I've seen the worse elected to Queen's Park. Remember Stuart Wideman, better known as Wildman Stu? What do you have against this guy?"

"You know better than anyone after spending all this time with him. This guy is a loose cannon. Obviously, Peter doesn't see it or doesn't want to see it. As far as I'm concerned, he should be relegated to the backbenches, never to be heard from or seen again. But I'm afraid that won't be happening."

The bartender has poured another round of vodka. Jerry

coughs as he throws it back. "Christ, how do you drink this stuff?"

"I gotta pee I'll be right back." Geneva gets up from her chair and just about falls over. "Oops. I've never been good in heels on a boat."

He looks at her in bewilderment. "What are you talking about?" But she is already gone and staggering to the ladies room in the back. When she returns, he notices that her hair looks as if it's been put under a hand dryer and her lipstick could have been applied by a four year old. "Geneva, why don't we call it a night? We've got a lot of stuff to deal with tomorrow. I plan to show up at the office in the morning."

"I'm fine." She suddenly topples forward and her head hits Jerry in the face. A little stunned by the head butt, he grabs her and straightens her up.

"I'm calling a cab and taking you home." He grabs her coat and puts it around her shoulders and directs her outside, after paying off her bar tab. He is a little shocked when he sees the size of the tab. She has done enough damage for one evening. Once outside, the cool air makes Geneva ever so slightly more alert. Although it's after midnight on a weekday, the sidewalk is busy with young people heading to one of the nightclubs on the street. The more popular clubs have lineups of people waiting to get in. Jerry feels the street pulsating from the electronic music played in the clubs. Fortunately the Entertainment District is always crawling with cabs. Within a couple of minutes, they hail one down and head to Geneva's condo at Harbourfront. When they arrive at her place, Jerry decides that she is in no shape to get up to her place on her own. He grabs her by the arm and brings her up to the twenty-second floor. Geneva manages to open the door and he escorts her inside.

He's not quite sure what to do next. So he decides to just

leave her on her bed to sleep it off. As they walk into Geneva's bedroom, Jerry has one arm around her and the other reaching for the light, when suddenly she reaches over, puts both arms around him and kisses him. Not just a little peck but a long, passionate kiss. His reaction is a combination of experiencing an adrenaline rush and being tasered. He notices that one of her hands has slipped down and is undoing his belt. He pulls back, "Umm...what are you doing?"

"What does it look like I'm doing? I'm drunk and horny. I need to get laid."

"I really don't think this is a good idea."

She pushes him onto the bed and wiggles out of her tight stretch denims and begins to grind into him. "Geneva, we need to talk." She ignores him.

The excitement of the day and the alcohol make the rest of the night a blur. The next thing Jerry remembers is rolling over early the next morning and seeing Geneva asleep next to him. "Holy shit, I just fucked my boss."

CHAPTER 14

**"Man does not control his own fate.
The women in his life do that for him."**
Groucho Marx

Jerry quietly gets out of bed, without disturbing Geneva, and gets dressed. He considers just sneaking out but decides that would be worse than facing up to what had happened the previous evening. Maybe he'll just leave a note. But what does he say?

'You were a great lay.'

'See you at work later today.'

How about 'I assure you this won't affect our working relationship'?

While considering the right words to use, he hears Geneva stirring in the bedroom. He finds her sitting on the edge of the bed holding her head in her hands and a sheet draped around her naked body. He forces a smile. "Good morning!"

She looks up at him with a face that expresses an epic hangover, horror and disgust. "What the fuck Switzer?"

"Look, no one needs to know anything about this. It will not affect our work relationship."

"You're damn right it won't affect our work relationship because you no longer work for me."

"You're firing me?"

"Don't get so dramatic. Let's just say you're getting a promotion to an executive assistant. But I'm not going to have you around the Premier's office."

"That's not fair."

"Welcome to life, Switzer."

She pulls the sheet tighter around herself as she gets out of bed. "By the way, thanks for escorting me home last night. Now clear out of here. I need to shower and get dressed."

Dejected and tired, he creeps out of her apartment and hails a cab, which takes him to the lot where he had left his car the night before in the Entertainment District. Since he's been shipped out of the Premier-elect's office with no official home, Jerry decides he is going to take some well-deserved time off. He heads home with the intention of sleeping the rest of the day. By the time he finally makes it back to his condo, his head is pounding. He grabs a couple of ibuprofen and crawls into his bed. Before he can even close his eyes, his phone begins to ring. He picks it up. "Hello."

"Hi, it's Rick. You disappeared early last night."

"Yes, I was out with a former colleague celebrating...let's just say things got a little out of hand. How are you doing? You must be on quite a high."

"Well things are starting to sink in. Yesterday was quite a shock, a happy one, but still shocking. I don't know squat about Queen's Park and I'm going to need some guidance. You're an old hand at this stuff so I'm thinking, since we have already been working together..."

"Rick, you will need to wait to see what role you are given. Your role in the government and caucus defines what staffing you are entitled to. Over the next few days, announcements will be made about Cabinet and then parliamentary assistants. But if you would like a head start on the orientation process, we can start with a tour of the Legislative Building. I've got some down time this week so if you are keen we can get together on Thursday."

"That would be great. How about late morning and then we can grab lunch?"

"Sure thing. See you then."

Even before the election, there was a lot of speculation regarding Cabinet posts but Rick notices that the rumor mill is in overdrive over the next few days. He has been told that when making appointments, Peter needs to consider regional representations, gender, minorities, experience and, of course, the people who got him elected. As far as Rick is concerned, he feels he played an important role in bringing voters to the party. The rumors he is hearing indicate that the auto insurance file, which he profiled during the election, albeit inadvertently, is coming his way. He is feeling a few butterflies fluttering around in his stomach, but the series of events since Peter first asked him to run has him feeling pretty good at the moment.

———

On Thursday morning, Jerry walks from his condo building just south of Queen's Park to the Legislative Building to meet up with Rick. The air is cold and damp from an overnight frost. As he walks down Wellesley Street, he passes a panhandler with two dogs sitting on a street corner. The man is dressed in khaki pants and an overcoat with a Blue Jays cap hiding much of his straggly hair. He has an unkempt beard and dirty hands holding up a sign. As he gets closer and able to read the sign, it elicits a chuckle from Jerry - NEED $$ FOR WEED. He pulls a loony out of his pocket and drops it in a pail placed on the sidewalk in front of the man. "I like your honesty."

"Thank you, kind sir!" the man responds.

Just ahead is Queen's Park Circle. The trees are almost bare and the groundskeepers are busy collecting the fallen leaves. Jerry's phone begins to ring. He glances down at the screen and rolls his eyes. "Hello Geneva."

"Jerry, as you may know a transition team was thrown together last week. Discussions have been finalized about Cabinet posts. Rick Tompkins has stuck the party with this twenty-five percent rate reduction commitment. It was decided that if he won his seat he could take the lead on the auto insurance file. So congratulations, you're going to be his EA."

"Why do I feel like I'm being shipped out to a Siberian gulag?"

"Aren't you being just a little dramatic? The Ferguson Block is hardly Siberia."

"I suppose."

"Keep this to yourself until it becomes official. Good luck with your new assignment. You'll need it." Then the line goes silent.

Jerry glumly continues his walk to the Legislative Building. He arrives at Queen's Park shortly before 10:30 a.m. and Rick is there standing under one of the three large stone archways that make up the front entrance to the building.

Rick is bursting with excitement and grabs Jerry's hand to shake. "Great to see you! Let's get started!"

Jerry forces a smile. "Good morning Rick and welcome to the 'Pink Palace'."

"Why do they call it the Pink Palace?"

"The exterior walls are made of pink sandstone quarried from the Credit Valley near Orangeville. Smog and dirt have darkened the stone but scrape away the outer surface and you will see that the stone is actually pink. Did you know the main entrance appeared on the cover of Rush's 1981 album Moving Pictures?"

Jerry takes Rick into the lobby and past the security detail at the main entrance. Rick pauses to gaze at how polished the oak floors and paneling in the lobby appear. Jerry leads him into the corridor and towards the stairs to the bottom floor. As they approach the staircase, Jerry turns to direct Rick's attention to the main entrance. "This building is actually the seventh structure to serve as Ontario's parliament building. The first parliament building was on Front Street and Berkeley Street. It was burned down in the War of 1812. This building opened on April 4, 1893. The grounds surrounding the building are Queen's Park; they are owned by the University of Toronto. The provincial Crown has a 999 year lease with the university that costs the province $1 per year. The lease runs out in 2892 so it's quite the deal."

"You must have worked as a tour guide here when you were a student."

"No, I'm just a bit of a history buff. In particular, anything involving parliamentary traditions really interests me."

"Can we see the Legislative Chambers?"

"That's on the second floor. Let me show you the other wings before we head upstairs. Two wings branch out from the center block that contains the Legislative Chamber. The east and west wings look quite different. If you look down toward the east wing, you can see the hallway has the original oak floors, oak paneling and cast iron columns. The west wing interior has Italian marble."

Rick stops and looks down the floor, "So it is. Why is that?"

"The west wing was badly damaged by a fire in 1909. When it was rebuilt, the exterior was kept the same but the interior was given a complete makeover with marble and stained glass. You can see Ontario's Coat of Arms in the skylight right above us."

"How did the fire start?"

"A spark from a charcoal burner used in roof repairs was blamed. The Legislative Library was completely destroyed, along with approximately 100,000 books and public records. I'll take you up to the Chambers."

They return to the center block and climb the grand staircase directly opposite, from the mid-landing which provides access to the Legislative Library in the 1909 block. At the top landing of the stairs is the lobby of the Legislative Chamber. A provincial police constable is stationed at the doors and is about to stop the two men when he recognizes Jerry as legislative staff. As they step inside, Rick pauses to take it all in. The room has intricate carved wood and plaster relief with carpeting and chair upholstery in green. "This place is much more impressive in person than on TV. Where will I sit?"

"The government sits on the right of the room and the opposition on the left side. Right in front of us is where the Sergeant-at-Arms sits. Directly in front of us is the Speaker's chair. Right above where the Speaker sits is the press gallery. You will quickly discover that members have a love/hate relationship with the media. On the sides are the public galleries."

Rick begins to fidget and finally jumps in, "What I really need is a tour of a local restaurant. I haven't had breakfast and I'm starving."

"Okay. There are a few decent places in the area. Although you will find it's often easiest just to run down to Quorum Café, which is right in the building."

They walk out the east entrance and head up to Wellesley Street and then east to Bay Street. They pick out a pub and sit down to order beer and sandwiches. The beers come first and Rick makes a toast "To four years of Conservative rule. Listen to me! I sound like such a politician. So where are you going to land? Are you heading back to work with Peter?"

"No, it appears that I'll be moving elsewhere."

"Why? I would think a guy like you would be itching to work in the Premier's office."

"It's time for a change of scenery."

Rick is about to press him further but his phone begins to ring. "Hi Peter." From the look on Rick's face, Jerry assumes he is getting the big news. "I really appreciate this opportunity and am very excited about taking the lead on this important work." After hanging up he returns to Jerry. "Peter has created a minister without portfolio for me, whatever that is."

"That's a Cabinet Minister without a ministry reporting to him."

"Peter said they are creating a secretariat to work on auto insurance reforms, for which I will be responsible. Isn't that like having a ministry?"

"It can be although the secretariat will likely be quite small. But it's a high profile file now and a great opportunity. Congratulations."

"Thanks. Just wondering, will I be able to continue running my insurance business on the side while working down here in Queen's Park?"

"No. You aren't going to have time. This is a full time gig. Also, since your portfolio involves insurance, you are going to have to set up a blind trust to avoid any conflict of interest."

Rick has a frown on his face. "That sucks."

Jerry forces a smile although he thinks it may not look very sincere. "Oh, I might as well tell you now. I'll be your executive assistant. So it looks like we'll continue working together, after all."

CHAPTER 15

"When you come to Parliament on your first day, you wonder how you ever got here. After that, you wonder how the other members got here." John Diefenbaker

It is parliamentary tradition that immediately following the Lieutenant Governor's acceptance of the formal resignation of an outgoing administration, the Premier-Designate signs a document recommending the appointment of ministers forming the new Cabinet, and assigning portfolios to those who will be in charge of a ministry. Rick is the only minister without a portfolio. The Lieutenant Governor's approval of this document accepts the recommendations and authorizes the taking of oaths as well as the commissions of appointment, which are subsequently prepared.

Rick is barely able to sleep the night before the swearing-in ceremony. Although he has never had any political ambition, now that he finds himself about to be appointed to Cabinet, he can barely contain his excitement. Lois, Jeremy and Kyle join Rick for the drive downtown to watch the ceremony. Don and Sylvia Brand, as well as Rick's parents, plan to attend as well. Although Don Brand still has doubts about his son-in-law, he is excited to have a Conservative Cabinet minister in the family. It's a cool and damp day but the weather has no effect on the twenty-four freshly elected MPPs who are to become the Executive Council, better known as the Cabinet.

The Tompkins and Brand families arrive about an hour before the start of the swearing-in ceremony, which will take place in the Legislative Chambers at 2:00 p.m. Rick's family heads up to the Public Gallery while Rick goes to Room 247, which is the Government Caucus Room, where the other future Cabinet ministers are congregating. The accredited press are allowed to position themselves just outside the Legislative Chamber and Caucus Room. The non-accredited media are sent up to the Press Gallery. The Caucus Room is bursting with energy and the occupants are continually being asked to keep the noise down. Some of the faces are new to the Conservative caucus, including Rick, and this is the first opportunity for introductions. Marco Pinto, the Finance Minister, approaches Rick to thank him for taking this "messy" file off his plate, since insurance matters normally reside under Finance.

Shortly before 2:00 p.m., the Sergeant-At-Arms knocks on the door and leads the procession of ministers into the Legislative Chambers, carrying the ceremonial Mace over his shoulder. The new Premier walks out first, followed by the Deputy Premier and then all the ministers in order of precedence which is determined by how long they have been an MPP. As a rookie MPP, Rick is the last person in the procession. After entering the Legislative Chamber, they are seated again in order of precedence. The Premier and every minister first take the Oath of Allegiance and Oath of Member of the Executive Council. Following that, the Premier and each minister with a portfolio take their individual oath of office. Since Rick has no ministry reporting to him, he sits and watches the other ministers take their individual oath. He gazes up at the Public Gallery, trying to find his family. He finally sees them and gives a short wave to his children. Next, the

Premier and the Lieutenant Governor sign the oaths. The clerk also signs as a witness, in his official capacity as a commissioner for taking affidavits.

The ceremony lasts less than an hour at which time the newly minted Cabinet members file out and head to the Cabinet Boardroom, which is off of the Premier's office. Here they have their first official meeting, which lasts less than one-half hour. Following this, Premier Lysiak emerges with his Cabinet colleagues to make a brief statement and answer questions from the media. Rick is watching the scrums as they quickly form around a minister and then just as quickly disappear and reappear around another one. One reporter makes eye contact with him and walks towards him. Rick recognizes her. "Hello Minister Tompkins, I'm Christie Lefebre, *Toronto Sun* reporter."

"Yes, I recognize you. How are you?"

"I'm fine. So congratulations on your successful campaign. I'm wondering if I could ask you a couple of questions."

"Go ahead."

"Word has it that you don't get along with the Premier's chief of staff, Geneva Horvath. I'm curious to know if there is any truth to that?"

"I don't know Geneva very well. I know she has a difficult job to do."

"And you don't particularly like her?"

"Well, let's just say I won't be inviting her up to the cottage for a couple of beers on the deck."

"Would that be because she is a woman?"

"No, it's because she is a first class bitch. Umm, I mean..."

"You have an issue with women that wield power. Admit it."

"Not at all. My wife wields plenty of power and I like her."

"But I'm more interested in hearing why you think Geneva Horvath is a bitch."

"Look, I've said too much. You will have to excuse me. I have some people waiting for me."

"All right, I'll leave it at that. Again congratulations, Minister Tompkins."

The media begin to leave to file their stories. Rick makes his way down from the second floor of the Legislative Building to the main lobby where his family has been waiting. Don has made reservations at Ruth's Chris Steak House to celebrate this special day.

———

Rick is eager to officially begin his new career at Queen's Park. He has been assigned an office on the fourth floor of Ferguson Block, a fourteen-story office tower that is part of a complex of government office buildings in the Bay and Wellesley area. A large black woman with short kinky hair is sitting at a desk outside his office. She looks up and greets him with a smile. "Good morning, Minister. I'm Barbara McKay, your executive secretary."

"Hello Barbara, nice to meet you. Who else is working here?"

"Jerry Switzer is in the office next to you. He's out at the moment. I understand there is a deputy minister. I don't know who it is. That's about it for now. Is there anything I can do for you at the moment?"

"I'm fine right now. I would like to get settled first." Rick walks into his office, which is facing north overlooking Wellesley Street. There is a large wooden desk that appears to have been around since the building opened in 1969. The walls are painted in a faded beige; about the same color as white paper left in the sun too long. On the walls are photos of Ontario wildlife:

snowy owls, beavers, white-tailed deer and blue jays. The office has a sitting area with a coffee table and some of the most uncomfortable looking chairs he has ever seen. Adjacent to the office is a small boardroom that seats about eight people around an oval wooden table. The boardroom has an entrance from the main reception area as well as one directly from Rick's office. Rick leans back in his chair and takes it all in. He likes the idea of wielding power.

Rick hears a knock at his office door and heads back inside. His executive assistant is peering inside. "Good morning, Jerry."

"Hi Rick, do you have a few minutes?"

"Sure, make yourself comfortable."

Jerry pulls up a chair in front of Rick's desk. "I've just returned from the Premier's office with word about a deputy minister appointment. Margaret Bouton will be the Deputy reporting to you. Margaret has been in the public service for about twenty-five years. This is her first deputy minister appointment. Previously, she has worked in Labour, Government Services, Finance and most recently Transportation, where she was an Assistant Deputy Minister. She is very competent and results-oriented. She has plenty of experience to assist someone like you. That is, someone new to government."

"Well, I'm looking forward to meeting with her."

"She will be showing up sometime this morning for a meet and greet with you. The government is creating an Auto Insurance Reform Secretariat to work with you on developing a set of reforms and a strategy for reducing rates by twenty-five percent. AIRS, which is what people inside are calling it, should be up and running in a couple of weeks as they draft staff from other ministries. The Secretariat will report to you through Margaret. You have been allocated resources for a communications coordinator and one policy advisor. Someone from Cabinet

Office has been recommended for the communications job. I am meeting with that person later today. I will find someone appropriate for the policy job."

"What about Ameena 3?"

"I thought she would be perfect to run your constituency office. She will be good at outreach and speaks Punjabi."

"Yeah, that makes sense. I will leave these things in your good hands."

Just then there is a knock on the door. They both turn in the direction of the knock and notice a tall, thin woman with short, grey hair standing at the door. She is wearing a dark blue pantsuit à la Hillary Clinton and no makeup. "Is this a good time?"

Rick jumps to his feet and grabs her hand to shake. "Please come in. I'm Rick Tompkins."

"It's a pleasure to meet you, Minister. I'm Margaret Bouton."

"Grab a chair Maggie. We were just chatting. And you can call me Rick."

"Thank you, Minister. However, my name is Margaret and not Maggie. I would prefer to keep things on a professional level."

"Sure."

"I am here to support you in any way I can to deliver the government's auto insurance promise. I spent some time in the policy division of the Ministry of Finance so I am somewhat familiar with the auto insurance file. I know this is very early in the process but I thought it might be helpful if you could summarize how you envision achieving your rate reduction target. What areas of the system do you see requiring reform? What do you see as the biggest obstacles? What time frame are you looking at for completing this work?"

"Actually Margaret, I haven't given this as much thought as you might think. Our focus until now has been on getting elected. I have to admit when I suggested that rates could be brought down by twenty-five percent, I had no plan on how to do it. I was expressing my gut feeling about the system based on nineteen years as a broker."

"Well, perhaps this is early to be getting into the weeds. I just wanted to introduce myself. I am recruiting Secretariat staff and will schedule a series of briefings to get you fully up to speed on the system, the legislation, the stakeholders and actuarial data. I will set up something with your office when we have pulled material together for you." She then gets up and shakes his hand again before sailing out of the office.

Rick turns to Jerry and rolls his eyes. "Hey Deputy Bow-Wow certainly has a bubbly personality."

At the end of the day, Jerry has squeezed in a brief meeting with his new communications officer. Jerry suggests that they meet at a Starbucks down the street, rather than at the office. It is raining and windy outside. Shortly after 5:00 p.m., Jerry grabs a sturdy umbrella for the walk to the cafe. Of course, sturdy umbrella is probably an oxymoron. When he walks into the cafe, he looks around and spots a tall, athletic young man with long blond hair and blue eyes sitting alone at a table. He is smartly dressed in tan slacks, a navy blazer and light blue oxford shirt. Jerry approaches him with an outstretched hand. "Hi, I'm Jerry Switzer. You must be Lawrence Tucker." His large hand engulfs Jerry's.

"Hi Jerry. I've heard a lot of good things about you. Looking forward to joining the team."

"Thanks. I'm ordering a coffee. Can I get you something?"

"I'd love a chai tea latte. I'm addicted to Starbucks chai tea latte."

"I'll be back with the drinks."

A few minutes later, Jerry returns with drinks and sits down. "So I understand you are, or at least you were, a big-time hockey prospect."

"Well, not that big. I went to Providence College with a hockey scholarship so I got my university education paid for. And I was the team's leading scorer in my senior year. In 2006, I was a seventh-round pick of the Nashville Predators and went to one of their tryout camps. But I didn't see myself playing professional minor league hockey. So here I am."

"Well, I'm glad you are. I'm sure you've heard this is an important file for the government."

"Yes."

"We also have a pretty green minister. He has a propensity for putting his foot in his mouth. In some cases, he doesn't stop at just one foot. So this position will not only involve communicating government policy but likely some damage control from time to time. I need someone who can sniff out trouble before it hits the fan, so to speak, and can turn around stuff pretty damn quick. I hope you're that person."

"I definitely am. I'm up for this."

"Good."

"I do have one question about the Minister."

Jerry is already frowning. "Go ahead."

"I've been hearing negative things about the Minister's views on race and sex."

"Well… I have to honest. He is far from politically correct. But the work environment is fine."

"I'm raising this because I happen to be gay. I don't want there to be any problems with my sexual orientation."

"I think you'll be fine. The environment can be weird at times but definitely not anything to be worried about."

"There is something else I'm curious about?"

"Okay."

"Doesn't the Minister come from the insurance industry?"

"Yes."

"Then shouldn't auto insurance reforms be a no-brainer for him? It should be like hiring a plumber to fix a leaky faucet."

"I wish it was that simple. The Minister sold insurance. He has no experience in reengineering projects, such as this one. He has a basic understanding of how the auto insurance product actually works. So to use your analogy, it would be like hiring the guy in the kitchen store who sold you the faucet to fix the leak."

"Okay, I guess that makes sense."

"Drop by tomorrow and we can start going over things." They chat a little more and then head home for the evening.

CHAPTER 16

**"If you don't know where you are going,
you'll end up someplace else." Yogi Berra**

The new Conservative government's Speech from the Throne is delivered by Lieutenant-Governor Muriel Patton several weeks later. The Speech contains a wide range of 'pocket book' commitments including tax cuts, reduced red tape, utility rate freezes and welfare controls. Of course, the central piece of the Speech is the commitment to lower auto insurance premiums. The only additional detail provided is an announcement that an Auto Insurance Reform Secretariat has been established to recommend a new auto insurance scheme within a year.

The next day's headlines are filled with news about the new government's agenda. One of Lawrence's jobs is to put a package of relevant news stories together and provide them to Rick and Jerry. Lawrence is receiving media requests for interviews with Rick, who has quickly developed the reputation of being a bit of a maverick. Since he is a political newcomer, reporters are eager to provide the public with a profile of the new minister. Of course, Rick is quite pleased with the maverick label.

Margaret Bouton spends the first few weeks recruiting staff for the new Secretariat. She also begins the process of hiring an independent actuarial consultant to assist in the technical aspects of the project. The Secretariat is located down the hall from Rick's office, in Ferguson Block. Based on her first meeting with the Minister, she understands that he has no real clue on how to bring about a major premium reduction. The government's promise for a new insurance scheme had no details or parameters. Therefore, her initial meetings with her new staff focus on developing a project plan. Essentially, a roadmap setting out where the government wants to get to, although the means of transportation have yet to be determined. A staffer has come up with a clever name for the project – *The Road Ahead*. The project plan calls for a consultation period to solicit ideas (since the Minister has none) followed by a period of policy analysis and development by staff.

When the project plan is complete, the Deputy Minister arranges for a briefing with Rick to get his sign off. Jerry and Lawrence attend the briefing as well as a senior staffer from the Secretariat, which is held in the Minister's boardroom.

Margaret is a little hesitant when she begins her presentation, knowing the plan is pretty much void of any detail. "Minister, I would like to run you through our initial thoughts about developing a package of reforms for the government. The one-year timeframe mentioned in the Throne Speech will be tight. We would have preferred two years."

"I think one year is more than doable."

"Yes, Minister. We understand the importance of this commitment and how it is a critical part of government's agenda. So let me walk you through our presentation and then we will be happy to hear your thoughts. My sense is that there is no firm plan on how to reduce premiums, which provides considerable flexibility. We believe the first step in the plan is to solicit ideas regarding cost saving approaches. This might include what type of compensation should be available, how insurance services should be delivered and how the product should be priced. We have prepared a list of stakeholder and interest groups who could be invited to provide you with submissions on how to make changes to the system, to bring down costs. This is the typical cast of characters who come out of the woodwork whenever auto insurance begins getting the government's attention." She distributes a stakeholder list to those around the table.

Rick frowns when he runs through the list. "Why are there legal groups on this list? I don't want to hear from those blood-sucking leeches."

"There are organizations and groups on the list that may not be supportive of possible changes. The government has to be seen as inclusive and open to listening to views that the government may not share. You are not obligated to act on what you are told but it's important that you provide everyone with the opportunity to be heard."

"Okay, we'll keep them on the list."

"We see the consultation phase lasting four months. Secretariat staff will receive the submissions and provide copies to you and your staff. We will follow up with face-to-face meetings with stakeholders to discuss their submissions. Those meetings will be set up by the Secretariat and we will coordinate with your scheduler. At the same time, the Secretariat will conduct a review of other jurisdictions to identify low cost auto insurance schemes and how they are structured."

Rick jumps in. "How will we know what changes should be made?"

"In the next phase, Secretariat staff will analyze all the information gathered from stakeholders and other jurisdictions and provide you with policy options. We are hiring an actuarial consultant to cost all these options and help identify where you can find twenty-five percent premium savings. I need to advise you that the target will be very difficult to achieve."

"Well, there is no flexibility on the target."

"Yes, we understand that. I am just forewarning you that some difficult decisions will need to be made."

Margaret looks down at her notes and continues. "The final phase is preparing a Cabinet Submission and getting policy approval from Cabinet. We've come up with a name for the project. We'd like to call it *The Road Ahead.*"

"Hey, I like that."

Jerry jumps in. "Lawrence, we will need a communications plan to develop some messaging on the project and manage issues, as they arise."

"Yes boss. I'll pull something together in the next few days."

Jerry turns to the Deputy Minister. "Thank you for pulling this together in such a short timeframe. I know there is going to be a lot of work for all of us over the next twelve months. I'm looking forward to the challenge. Rick, do you have any other questions for Margaret?"

"Nothing at the moment. Can't wait to get rolling."

With that, the meeting breaks up. Rick has an interview scheduled with *Toronto Sun* reporter Christie Lefebre. She is calling in about twenty minutes. Just enough time to grab some coffee from the Tim Hortons on the main floor of the building. In the lobby, on the way back to the office, he runs into Lawrence who is carrying back a chai tea latte to his office. Rick stops him. "How's it going, Larry?"

"I go by Lawrence."

Rick is smirking as he repeats the name. "Okay then, Lawrence it is. Though you know, big guy, it makes you sound a little gay.

"I am gay."

"No shit! I hear you were a stud scorer at some U.S. college."

"That's right. I went to Providence College on a hockey scholarship."

"Jeez. I would never have guessed. The gay part, that is. But I'm cool with it. Whatever floats your boat, man."

At this point, Lawrence lets out a sigh. "Thanks."

Rick nods and returns to his office. Barbara calls to let him know the reporter is on the line. "Good morning, this is Rick Tompkins."

"Good morning, Minister. Thank you so much for making yourself available. Your election success and profile have created a lot of public interest. The *Sun* would like to do a profile of you for this weekend's paper."

"Sounds good to me."

"I have your bio so we can skip chatting about your background. Let me start by asking you about when you became interested in politics."

"I've been friends with Peter Lysiak for years. Earlier this year, he convinced me to run in my home riding. I thought about it and took the plunge."

"That riding hasn't got much of a reputation for electing Conservatives to office. Did you actually believe you could win?"

"I don't care about pollsters and pundits. I know the people in my riding and they were ready for a change "

"So, is that why you raised the car insurance issue during the campaign?"

"I knew it was an important issue in Brampton. It needed to be raised. I'm not afraid to speak out."

"So, you like being labelled a maverick?"

"I kind of like it. It fits my personality."

"Well, you changed the entire direction of the election. Is it possible that you saddled the government with a commitment it can't deliver?"

"I am confident we can deliver."

"Any insights on what changes the public can expect?"

"We are early in the process and have a lot of people to talk to. The sector is full of smart people and we want to hear from them all."

"Your campaign was supported by volunteers from your brokerage firm. Some of the women who helped you seemed to have attracted a lot of attention. Any comments on the attention they received?"

"The girls put in a lot of volunteer hours. That's the part people seem to miss. I'm very appreciative of all the time everyone on my team put in to get me elected."

"Thank you, Minister. I think we have enough here. The only thing I would like to arrange is a photo to go with the article. I'd like to come over perhaps tomorrow with a photographer to take some shots of you in your office."

"Sounds good. Since you brought up Ginny and Brittney, I thought maybe we could include them in the shot. It would be my way of thanking them for their help. I know they would get a kick out of being in the Sun."

The reporter cannot believe the gift she has been presented with. She attempts to hide her enthusiasm, although she is beaming. "Sure. We can take a few photos with and without them. We'll see what works best. I'll call your assistant and set up a time."

The next day Christie Lefebre shows up with a photographer. Ginny and Brittney are already there with Rick. The photographer takes a series of shots of Rick at his desk and then a few shots with the women sitting at the edge of his desk. A few are taken in his boardroom sitting around the table. As she leaves, Christie lets them know the profile will be published in the Sun's Sunday edition.

———

Lawrence is getting fidgety waiting at the restaurant bar for Ameena 3 to show up. He is playing with his phone and trying not to finish his drink too quickly. He gets a text from her.

I'm almost there. Just looking for a parking spot.

Several minutes later, he sees a petite Indian woman walk into the restaurant. Lawrence waves in her direction until she spots him. He gets up to hug Ameena 3.

"I'm sorry I'm so late. It's crazy busy trying to set up the constituency office and then the traffic coming in from Brampton is horrendous."

"It's quite all right. I'm glad you agreed to meet with me. Do you want to sit at the bar or should we get a table?"

"The bar works for me."

"As I mentioned over the phone, I know this communications position will be a challenge. Any insight you can give me from when you worked on the campaign would be helpful. Can I order you a drink?"

"I would love one. I feel like a tequila sunrise."

Lawrence gestures to one of the bartenders who takes their orders for drinks and appetizers. He gets back to their conversation. "So how did you get involved in Rick Tompkins' campaign?"

"I've known Jerry Switzer from the time I started doing work for the Conservative Party. He brought me into the campaign, which was a bit of a pain because I live in downtown Toronto. And now I run Rick's Brampton constituency office but I'm getting used to the commute."

"I'm interested in what you can tell me about the Minister."

Ameena 3 struggles to come up with the right words. "Well… he's not your typical politician."

"In what way?"

"I think for someone in the public spotlight, he's a little rough around the edges."

Lawrence smirks at the description. "Oh yes, his lack of tact."

Ameena 3 responds. "Other than being a misogynistic, racist homophobe, he's just fine!" They both break out laughing.

"Oh my god! He adds in a hushed voice, "When I told him my name was Lawrence, he told me that sounded gay. So I told him I was gay. You should have seen the look on his face. How did you deal with it?"

They begin to laugh again. "He needs to be very scripted and then you hope he sticks to the script." Trying to look serious, she adds: "I think you're going to learn a lot about crisis management. Jerry will provide a lot of guidance and I'm always available to help. We're all part of the same team."

Lawrence raises her glass and clinks it with Ameena 3's. "Here's to four years of Rick Tompkins."

ses for technology to catch up to the conversation.

en the explosion. "What the fuck is wrong with that

e have given the lead on the government's biggest policy

ve to a sexist moron!"

Who you dumped on me to kill my career."

That is your own doing. You're lucky you aren't working as

e in the Legislature."

"So how should we be handling this? I guess we'll be getting

d out on this during Question Period."

"I'll get Cabinet Office to prepare a house note for the

mier. It might be advisable for Minister Shit for Brains to be a

show' for house duty tomorrow. As for those two lovely tarts,

rhaps we should arrange to have them relocated to Nipigon.

rmanently." Then the line goes dead.

Jerry's next call is to Rick but before he can dial the number,

is phone is ringing. "Hi Mom. How are you?"

"I have to call you so that you can ask me how I am?"

He sighs and takes a breath. "Of course not. You do remember I just saw you a couple of days ago."

"You have elderly parents. A few days can make a big difference. Last week, Ben Cooper was taking groceries out of the car and dropped dead in the garage. Massive heart attack."

"Seriously? Ben Cooper? He wasn't that old."

"I know. His wife comes out to find out what's taking him so long. Maybe he's got caught up in a conversation with a neighbor. The poor woman finds him next to the car with two kosher chickens by his side."

"That's too bad. Did you call me to tell me about Ben Cooper?"

"Oh no. I forgot to tell you when you were last over that next Friday night is the start of Hanukkah. Everyone is coming over for *latkes*."

CHAPTER 17

"Scandal is gossip made tedious by morality."
Oscar Wilde

On Sunday mornings, Rick, Lois and the boys always head out for brunch at their favorite breakfast place just bordering Brampton, in the northern part of Mississauga. It's an old-style diner with greying linoleum tiles on the floor, a beige Formica counter and red checkered table clothes. The bills are handwritten and when you're done, you pay the cashier at the front of the restaurant. Rick always orders bacon (well done), eggs (sunny side up), and hash browns. This morning is no different. Lois orders an egg white omelet and brown toast. Jeremy and Kyle are having waffles with syrup. On the way into the restaurant, Rick picks up a copy of the *Toronto Sun*. He flips through the paper and finds the article on page 7 and begins reading it to his wife. When done, he looks up from the paper. "I like what she's done. I had Ginny and Brittney show up for the photo session and they used a shot with them. What do you think?" He hands the paper over to Lois. He notices a frown appear on her face. "What's wrong?"

"Rick, this photo is incredibly sexist! The women are sitting on your desk each grabbing hold of one of your arms. They are wearing super tight skirts and showing tons of cleavage. And that smirk on your face makes you look like a dirty old man. It looks like you're about to have a ménage à trois."

"I don't think so."

Jeremy grabs the paper from his mother's hands. "Whoa, Dad! Who are they?" Kyle leans over his brother's shoulder to see what the fuss is about. He doesn't make a sound but his red cheeks give away what he is thinking."

"You see? Is this what you want your children to see?"

"I don't see the problem."

"Really Rick! Don't you ever learn? Haven't the media already beaten you up over these two women?"

"That was just campaign nonsense. The election is over. No one cares about that stuff anymore. The focus now is what we are doing at Queen's Park."

"Rick, the opposition parties are always looking for something to attack the government or individual ministers over. You may have made yourself a target."

The server has returned with their breakfast and is placing the plates down onto the table. The newspaper has been left open on the page with Rick's article. The server looks down and shouts out. "Hey, isn't that you in the paper?"

"Yeah, that's me," he says with a big grin.

"Nice looking babes. Are they strippers?"

Kyle turns red again. Lois glares at her husband. "You see?"

———

In his downtown Toronto condo, Jerry is enjoying a lazy Sunday morning. He is sprawled on his sofa watching a Sunday morning news program over coffee. In his hand is a copy of *The*

Road Ahead consultation announcement th released this week. Margaret Bouton had s his review before it gets sent to the Minister phone begins to ring. "Morning Lawrence, wh

"Have you seen the Minister's profile in to

"Nope. What's it say?"

"The issue isn't what it says. You need to see a pag used."

"What about the photo?"

"Hang on, I'm going to scan it and send it to when you get it."

"Okay." They hang up and Rick gets back to program. About a minute later, an email arrives from with an attachment. Jerry opens the attachment and scream at no one in particular. He calls Lawrence. "Oh how come we didn't know about this?"

"We knew the *Sun* was doing a profile. He had his sp points with him. I have no idea how the women showed up photo shoot. I didn't know they were going to include a ph That was never discussed with me."

"This is fucking terrible. The Legislature is in session a this is going to come up in Question Period, likely tomorrow. need to alert the Premier's Office."

"Well good luck. Let me know if there is anything I can do to help."

"Thanks. Bye."

He dials Geneva's number. "Switzer, what has you calling on a Sunday morning? Shouldn't you be getting some beauty sleep?"

"Cut the sarcasm. We have an issue to manage."

"Oh? What has Mr. Potato Head done now?"

"I'm sending you a photo that appears on page 7 of today's *Toronto Sun*. As they say, a picture is worth a thousand words."

"Friday is not good for me. The Secretariat is having their Christmas party that evening."

"That's fine. Go celebrate the holidays with the *goyem*."

"Look, I have to make an appearance at this party and then I'll head over to your place. Save some *latkes* for me. I've got to run. See you on Friday."

Jerry goes back to calling Rick, who is driving home from brunch with Lois. "Rick it's Jerry. I expect you've seen today's *Toronto Sun*."

"Yes. I'm guessing that since you are calling on a Sunday morning, this is not good."

"That is correct. This is not good. I expect the Opposition will be calling for you to be fired tomorrow."

"Really?"

Jerry is no longer hiding his annoyance as he shouts into the phone. "Rick, that's the way it works at Queen's Park! It's about discrediting the government in any way possible. Any indiscretion by a minister is going to be jumped on and blown into a big scandal. You need to stop doing stuff like this."

"Don't you Jewish people have connections in the media? Can't you call someone to make this go away?"

"No Rick, I can't make this go away," he sighs, ignoring another one of Rick's racial stereotypes, which he has become somewhat accustomed to by now. "I'm waiting to hear from Geneva. I'll let you know what the plan is first thing tomorrow morning. Enjoy the rest of your day while mine is going down the toilet."

Jerry slumps back on his sofa, returning to his TV which has been on mute for almost an hour. He wonders how he will survive these next four years working with a minister with no political experience and few political instincts. How can this minister possibly survive, behaving like this? Maybe that's a good thing. The government can survive the loss of a minister. Perhaps someone more competent will also be able to deliver on a significant policy commitment. The news is doing a story about Canadian hockey players playing in Russia. Right now, Vladivostok doesn't sound so bad.

———

When Rick steps out of the elevator onto the 4th floor on the Monday morning, he notices that elves have been busy at work over the weekend. The hallway leading to the Secretariat office has been decorated with tinsel and garland. There is a Christmas tree in the reception area just outside his office. As he walks by Barbara, he greets her and grins. "Merry Christmas Barbara."

She has been hovering around his office waiting for him. "Good morning, Minister. Jerry Switzer says he needs to speak to you immediately,"

Rick can hear Jerry on the phone from outside his office. "Thank you, Barbara. Tell him to come by when he's free."

Moments later, Jerry appears and sits down opposite Rick. "Here is the plan. You don't show up today for Question Period. You have some conflicting commitments. The premier will handle any Opposition questions regarding yesterday's *Sun* article. Also, if the media calls, you aren't available. Got it?"

"Yeah." Rick is relieved that he will be avoiding a grilling from the Opposition. In his short time as an MPP, he has already seen some nasty exchanges.

"As for the announcement that we are beginning our consultation process, that will have to be delayed by one week. By then the media and public will have moved on to some other issue. I'm heading over for Question Period. I suggest you watch it from your TV."

"Okay. Thanks for your help." Rick isn't sure Jerry even heard him as he is out the door before Rick can respond. He slumps back in his seat feeling a little dejected. As far as he's concerned, people are making a big deal out of nothing.

Question Period is still over an hour from now but Jerry decides to head over early. He makes his way to Wellesley Street and turns right towards the Legislative Building. The cool fall air makes him shiver but he knows that he will warm up quickly in the hot and stuffy Legislative Building. He can take the tunnels that connect many of the government buildings in Queen's Park but that always takes longer. He passes Whitney Block, which houses Cabinet Office and the Premier's Office. Each time he passes the building, it's a reminder of how he got stuck working for a dysfunctional minister instead of working for the Premier. He crosses Queen's Park Circle and enters the Legislature through the east entrance. He flashes his badge to the OPP officer stationed at the entrance and makes his way to one of the public galleries in the Legislative Chamber. Some members begin to appear and take their places, since the House is in recess until 10:30 a.m. Government members sit to the right of the Speaker and Opposition members to the left. The gallery also begins to fill with visitors, guests and reporters.

When the session is about to start, the main doors open and the Sergeant-at-Arms, carrying the Mace over his shoulder, leads a procession into the Chamber. The Speaker, Clerk, Table Clerks and two Legislative pages follow the Sergeant-at-Arms. Once in the Chamber, the Mace is placed on the Clerk's table with the crown end pointing towards the Government. The Sergeant-at-Arms bows to the Speaker, and proceeds to his desk near the entrance of the Chamber. The Speaker reads the prayer for the day, and the session begins.

Today's session begins with Question Period. The first

person to rise with a question is the Leader of the Opposition, Lawrence Shedden, who was Premier until losing the last election. "My question is for the Premier. I was shocked when I opened up a copy of the *Toronto Sun* yesterday and saw a photo of your Minister responsible for Auto Insurance Reform sitting at his desk, which was adorned by two young women." He pauses and holds up a copy of the *Sun* photo. "This appears to be a recurring issue with the Minister. As a father of two daughters, this distresses me. In several weeks, it is the National Day of Remembrance and Action on Violence Against Women. This day is dedicated to the memory of the fourteen women killed at L'École Polytechnique in Montreal on December 6, 1989. It is also a time to raise awareness that violence against women continues to exist in communities throughout Ontario and the rest of Canada. In light of his poor attitude toward women, is the Premier prepared to ask for the resignation of the Minister?"

The question is followed by calls of "here, here!" and the sound of fists pounding on desks from Opposition members. To Jerry, this always feels like a staged show. In fact, that's exactly what it is. No matter the issue, the Opposition is looking to discredit the Government and will invariably demand for the resignation of a minister. The Government, not wanting to appear weak, will defend the minister. Not that ministers don't get fired, but the Government would never want to give the appearance that it is giving in to the Opposition. The Premier rises to respond. "The Government takes the issue of violence against women very seriously. We plan to recognize the tragedy that occurred at L'École Polytechnique on December 6th. I have known the Minister for a long time and he is supportive of women's issues and respected in the community. It is the *Toronto Sun* who, in fact, has a reputation for exploiting women and this is just another example. I will not be asking the Minister to resign."

As he returns to his seat, the Chamber is again filled with vocal support and desk banging but this time from the Government side. The Opposition Leader is again recognized by the Speaker. "A supplementary question for the Premier. I look across to the Government's side of the Chamber and don't see the Minister responsible for Auto Insurance Reform. I would have liked to hear from him directly on this matter. Where is the Minister?"

The Premier again rises with a response. "Unfortunately, the Minister has conflicting commitments and could not be here today. But he has, on several occasions, expressed his support on women's issues. This is already a matter of public record and needs no rehashing in the House." Jerry lets out a sigh of relief as questions turn to other matters. The Opposition took their shots but they know there is little value in flogging this one further.

Later in the afternoon, Rick receives a call directly from Peter Lysiak. "Hi Rick. How are you making out?"

"Well, I thought I was doing pretty good until this *Sun* article blew up."

"A word of advice. Politics is a rough game. You've got all kinds of people looking to trip you up. We've been friends for a long time. I've got your back but if you become a liability, well, I will have to do what's best for the party. You've got to keep your nose clean."

"I hear you, Peter. Thanks for backing me up."

CHAPTER 18

**"Faith is not a political strategy and
should not be a political strategy." John Edwards**

Ameena 3 has arranged for Rick's inaugural quarterly BGM town hall that evening, at a local community center. When he walks into the center's multipurpose room, Ameena 3 rushes over to greet him. "Hello Boss. Glad you made it a little early so I can go over a few things with you."

They sit down in a corner of the room and Rick begins to whine. "I have no clue what this is about. Why do I have to show up for these things? I thought you were handling constituency stuff."

"Yes Boss, I am dealing with constituency issues. But voters want to be able to interact with you directly. It's important to reach out to the community between elections if you want to win the next election."

"Yeah, yeah. I got it. And stop calling me Boss."

"Yes Boss. This is going to be informal. You sit in the front and constituents who show up will get an opportunity to ask you questions or talk about problems they are having in dealing with government. You talk about what the government is doing. For those that raise a problem that needs to be resolved, I will get their contact info and follow up. Does that sound okay?"

"I've got it."

"Jerry has told me to remind you that you are not to stray off from the party's agenda. No freelancing."

"Okay already! I said I got it!"

"Thanks Boss."

"Stop calling me Boss!" People begin to fill the seats in the room. Rick turns to Ameena 3. "There isn't a white face in the room. I could have sworn when I was canvassing I saw white voters in the riding."

"The meeting notice goes out in an email blast to those on our voters list and is advertised in the ethnic newspapers. This is who turns out."

"Shouldn't we invite some white people too? For some balance?"

"Oh my god, I hope you're not serious." Ameena 3 decides to start the meeting. About thirty people are scattered around the room. "Good evening friends and neighbors. Welcome to Minister Tompkins' first riding town hall meeting. I am Ameena 3, manager of the Minister's constituency office, and I will be facilitating tonight's meeting."

An elderly man from the back of the room yells out. "You must be a very positive and optimistic person to have chosen the number 3 in your name. Well done." People in the room applaud.

"Yes, thank you. To continue, I thank you for coming out tonight. This is an opportunity to ask your Member of Parliament questions about the government and how he can help you. So Minister, if you are ready, we can begin." Rick nods his head.

Rick rises to say a few remarks. "I want to thank you all for coming out this evening. When the formal portion of the meeting concludes, I will be sticking around for a while and hope to get to meet some of you personally." He looks over to Ameena 3 who gives him a nod. "I'm not going to say too much because I want to make sure you people get a chance to speak. It's been three months since the election and the Conservative government has been quite busy. We've announced a tax cut. In a few months, we will table our first budget, which includes a plan to eliminate the provincial deficit in four years. We have announced that we will freeze the salaries of government workers, hydro rates, and welfare payments. We also develop a plan to lower auto insurance rates by twenty-five percent. As many of you know, I have been asked by the Premier to head up this very important project. The drivers in this riding will hopefully get some rate relief in a year from now. He pauses as the audience responds with enthusiastic applause. "So who has a question?"

Rick acknowledges a stooped elderly woman in the front wearing a blue saree. "Congratulations on your election victory, Minister. I am Manisha, a new Canadian, and have a number of health issues. Unfortunately, I have been waiting nearly a year for health insurance coverage so that I can see a doctor. What can you do to expedite my situation?"

Rick hesitates and looks over to Ameena 3. "Umm, yes that is a good question. My assistant Ameena 3 will get your contact information and follow up with you."

She nods her head and smiles. "Thank you, Minister Tompkins."

Next to ask a question is a tall, thin middle-aged man in a dark grey business suit with matching grey hair. "Minister Tompkins, my name is Raj Rathnam. I have been a personal injury lawyer in Brampton for nineteen years and my clients are concerned about your announced plans to reduce auto insurance premiums. As much as they want relief from cripplingly high premiums, they want to make sure they are still protected, should they be seriously injured by a reckless at-fault driver. Can you say anything to address their concerns?"

"Mr. Rathnam, thank you for coming out tonight and for your question. I hear what you are saying. We do not plan on making innocent accident victims pay for the reduction in premiums that we have planned for. We have begun a year-long process to identify how to produce those savings so that everyone benefits." The lawyer frowned but sat down without pursuing his question further.

Next Rick deftly handles questions about licensing drivers, gas taxes, congestion on 400 series highways and hospital emergency room crowding. Ameena 3 gives the floor to another woman who is also traditionally dressed. "Minister Tompkins. We see your picture in the newspaper. It is very disrespectful. You are a married man yet being seen with these women. You are disrespecting your wife."

"Oh no. These women work for me. It's fine with my wife."

A man jumps to his feet. "Why do you not have a picture taken with you wife?"

"I don't think you understand. These women worked on my campaign, which is why I had the picture taken. It has nothing to do with my wife."

Suddenly everyone in the room is talking at once. Rick turns to Ameena 3 and mouths the word 'help'. She shouts out to him. "Hey Boss, your first town hall turned out pretty well."

———

The Opposition parties quickly lose interest in the issue although letters from women's groups continue to trickle in. Jerry suspects that the *Sun* article and photo might have been an ambush. Scandals for reporters are the equivalent of a hanging curveball for a home run hitter. It's not something you pass up on. You want to hit it out of the park. Several days after the article is published, he decides to call up the reporter for an informal chat. "Good morning Christie, it's Jerry Switzer in Minister Tompkins' office."

"Good morning, Jerry. What can I do for you?"

"I wanted to thank you for the excellent profile you did on the Minister. I think it pretty much captures what he is about. But I'm curious how you went about selecting the photo that went with the article. I don't see how it is consistent with the theme of your article."

"I've been following Rick Tompkins from the early days of his campaign."

"Yes, I remember you from one of the candidates' meetings."

"There is a lot of public interest in the new government and in particular your Minister who is outspoken and unorthodox. He doesn't exhibit the qualities of a typical politician, which makes him stand out. But there are those that find some of his attitudes a little disturbing. It's my job to paint a complete picture for our readers."

"But your choice of photo distorts that picture. In fact, suggesting that the Minister pose with his firm's employees in his government office can imply something that isn't necessarily true."

"I never suggested taking that photo. The Minister proposed involving the two women in the photo shoot. We went along with it and published it because it reflects a mindset by the Minister that people should be and, in fact are, interested in."

Jerry lets out a long sigh. "Are you telling me that this was his idea?"

"Absolutely. I think it complements the profile very well despite your view that it is inconsistent."

"Thank you for sharing this with me. You have a nice day."

The conversation only angers Jerry that much more. It reinforces his view that the next four years will be difficult. He had been looking forward to a significant role in the government side of the House. Now that he has achieved that, he finds it's not all it's cracked up to be. Babysitting an unpredictable minister is not how he had envisioned public service.

The weekly caucus meeting is to start shortly and the reforms consultation is on the agenda. Jerry needs to hustle over to the Legislative Building if he is to get there in time. He speed walks across Wellesley Street and picks it up to a sprint across Queen's Park Circle, against the light while dodging traffic. Exercise is not a part of his routine so by the time he makes it past the security detail and up to Room 247, he is quite out of breath. He heads to the back of the room and of course the only seat available happens to be right next to Geneva.

"What's with you? Why are you breathing so hard?"

"I decided to take up jogging between meetings."

"Good idea. You need to be in shape to keep up with Minister Casanova."

Jerry is about to respond but the caucus meeting begins. The room is quite crowded and Jerry wonders how, in the past, caucuses of eighty members or more were able to squeeze into the room. The first agenda item is an update on auto insurance reform. Rick is asked to summarize the project plan for caucus members, which he reads from notes prepared by Jerry. "I am pleased to provide you will the details of our plan to deliver lower car insurance premiums to Ontario drivers by next year. The Auto Insurance Reform Secretariat is now set up and staffed and will be working with me on the review. The initial phase in our plan is to solicit ideas regarding cost saving approaches from our industry partners and stakeholders. The consultation phase will last four months. I will also hold face-to-face meetings with stakeholders to discuss their submissions. In the next phase, the Secretariat will analyze all the information gathered from stakeholders and other jurisdictions and develop policy options. The last step will be bringing a final proposal to Cabinet for policy approval. Are there any comments or questions?"

"Klara Panchyk, Mississauga West." The woman who gets to her feet is large-boned with big thick hands, more like a man than a woman. She is wearing a navy blue pant suit and thick gold jewelry around her neck and wrists. "Can you provide any insight on how a twenty-five percent rate reduction will be achieved? I hear from some constituents who are questioning how the government can possibly reduce rates this much."

"The consultations will help identify how best to achieve the rate reduction."

"But surely you have some idea on how this is going to be achieved. After all, this was a major campaign promise."

"I know it can be done. Right now we just need to figure out the details."

Before sitting down, she looks around the room. "Does anyone else in caucus feel somewhat uncomfortable about this?"

Next to get up is a large man who looks more like a backwoodsman than a politician. He has curly black hair, a thick beard and a ruddy complexion. "Jay Breem, Nipissing—Timiskaming. Will my constituents in the North see the same rate reduction as drivers in the Toronto area? Many of them feel that they are subsidizing Toronto drivers."

"Well, we haven't really thought about how the reduction will be applied."

"I just want to be on record as stating that I expect northern drivers to receive the same twenty-five percent savings as Toronto drivers." There is a smattering of applause as he sits back down.

"Darwin Chan, Scarborough-Centre. Is this going to be

another fraud witch hunt? The previous governments made a big deal about fraud, made a bunch of changes and rates never went down. If we are going to be making changes, I expect drivers to actually see their rates go down."

"Darwin, we haven't even started our review yet so I can't really tell you if fraud is a problem in the system. But I think we have been clear that drivers are going to see their rates go down."

The next MPP to comment is the most senior member of caucus and the party Whip. No one messes with him. Not only does he schedule the introduction of bills and votes but he also ensures there are always enough votes to pass a bill. "Blake Murdoch, Bruce-Grey-Owen Sound." The elderly politician has an impatient tone. "I'm hearing all these questions but no answers. Does anyone know what's going on with this file?"

The question is followed by grumbling from around the room at which point Peter Lysiak stands up to address caucus. "Look people, this is the early stages of the reform process. I am confident that as the review unfolds, Rick will have lots of information to pass along. My office will be sending out an information sheet with some facts about the review and how interested parties can become involved. We will also provide some messaging to ensure that you can answer questions from your constituents."

Caucus members begin to turn their attention to the next agenda item dealing with a transit infrastructure initiative. Jerry turns to Geneva. "Wow, this is just caucus. What's going to happen when this comes up during Question Period?"

CHAPTER 19

**"I went to a fight the other night,
and a hockey game broke out."
Rodney Dangerfield**

"Kyle, are you getting yourself psyched for today's game?" Kyle rolls his eyes and turns up the volume on his iPod. Rick looks at his son in his rearview mirror and realizes he is being ignored. "Kyle?"

Lois cuts in. "Rick, stop putting pressure on him. Don't ruin the experience of playing hockey. It's about having fun."

"What can be more fun than winning?"

"Seriously? He's just playing Peewee AA."

"You're right. We should have the boys on both teams form a healing circle at center ice, hold hands and sing Kumbaya."

There are few signs of life so early on a Sunday morning. Most of the homes they pass are still in darkness. There are only a small number of cars on the road. No doubt also heading to an arena somewhere. A light snow is falling, which is being blown around by the wind. Rick turns into the parking lot of Garnet A. Williams Arena in Vaughan. The fresh layer of snow on the ground makes a crunching sound under the tires of their SUV. Rick finds a parking spot as close to the entrance as he can. He opens up the hatch and pulls out a hockey bag and two sticks, which he hands over to Kyle. As they walk towards the arena entrance, the door flies open and Coach Ron is there to greet them. "Good morning folks. Kyle, we're in dressing room seven."

Kyle plods down the dressing room hallway dragging his bag over his shoulder. Lois calls out, "Good luck, Kyle."

Rick turns to the coach. "Hey Coach. I've got some ideas for today's game. I've noticed that the Panther's goalie is tall and doesn't move well from side to side. We need to get him moving in his crease. If we can get him out of position, I think it will create some good scoring chances."

Ron smiles. "Thanks for the advice, Rick. Enjoy the game." He turns away to greet another family who has just arrived.

Lois grabs Rick by the arm. "Let's grab some coffee at the snack bar."

Out in the lobby there are groups of parents standing around talking hockey over arena coffee. The dads and moms have formed separate little groups. It sometimes has the feel of a high school dance. The smokers are huddled outside in the parking lot doing the same. One dads yells out when he sees Tompkins walk in. "Hey Rick! Look at you with the fancy Mississauga Rebels team jacket."

Rick smirks. "That's right. I'm not ashamed to be seen supporting our boys!"

Another dad jumps in. "Rick, what happened to your Maple Leafs last night? Maybe you should give up politics and coach the Leafs."

"You know Greg, once I save you some money on your insurance, maybe I'll just do that."

"You couldn't possibly do worse."

When the players make their way out for their warm up, all the parents make their way into the rink. The Mississauga parents occupy one end of the rink and the Vaughan parents are on the other end. The Mississauga Rebels are in their away jerseys: white with blue trim. The Vaughan Panthers are wearing red jerseys with blue and gold trim. Following the three-minute warm up, the referee signals for a faceoff at center ice. Rick screams, "Let's GOOOO Rebels!"

The Vaughan team is just a little larger and quicker than Mississauga. The Rebels are pinned in their own end for the first two minutes of the game. A Rebel player is called for hooking and on the ensuing power play, the Panthers score. Rick stands up and shouts. "Let's get it back boys!" Kyle plays left wing and each time he has the puck in the Panthers' end of the ice, Rick is yelling for him to shoot the puck.

By the end of the first period, Vaughan is up by a score of 2-0. After a one minute break, the teams change ends and the referee signals for another faceoff at center ice. Vaughan wins the faceoff and one of their wingers dumps the puck into the Mississauga end and chases after it. A Rebel defenseman on that side of the ice turns around and also chases after it. The two players reach the puck at the same time and collide in the corner. The Mississauga defenseman is knocked down and is lying on the ice in obvious pain. One of the referees blows his whistle to stop the play. Rick stands up in a rage. "What the hell ref? That should be a major penalty!" The Mississauga trainer comes onto the ice and helps the injured boy off the ice. Rick can't believe no penalty is called. He runs to the boards next to where one of the referees is standing and begins to bang on the glass with his fists. "Hey ref, are you on the Vaughan payroll? You are a fucking disgrace."

Lois comes down to where Rick is standing. "Please sit down and stop making a scene."

He ignores her and continues to yell. So she grabs him by the arm and drags him back to where they were sitting. One of the parents jokes. "Take it easy Rick. This isn't Queen's Park."

When the Panther player involved in the collision comes back on the ice, Rick jumps to his feet and begins shouting again. "Somebody go out there and hammer number six! Come on boys, it's payback time!" The next time the player returns to the ice, Rick begins to repeat the abusive taunts. A man with curly brown hair and wearing a Vaughan Panthers hockey jacket walks over to where Rick is standing. He is well over six feet tall and weighs at least 250 pounds. His dark brown eyes are locked in on Rick. "Hey dickhead, that's my kid you're yelling at."

"Well, he's a goon."

The Vaughan dad is visibly agitated. "Why don't you sit down and shut the fuck up?"

"Why don't you turn around and head back to your end of the rink?"

"Why don't you make me, you little fucking dickweed?" He moves right up to Rick until Rick's eyes are directly even with the eyes of the Panther crest on his chest. Rick pokes the Vaughan giant in the chest with his finger. In response, he shoves his chest into Rick causing him to fall backwards.

Three dads jump in to rescue Rick. They literally pick him up and drag him out into the lobby. Greg looks at Rick in bewilderment. "Are you crazy? That guy could rip you in two."

"I'm not intimidated by that gorilla."

Suddenly Lois appears. "Rick, are you alright?"

"Yes, I'm fine."

"Good. What the hell is wrong with you? You could have gotten hurt. And don't you think your behavior is an embarrassment to Kyle?"

"Why? Because I stood up for myself? What's wrong with that?"

"No, because you acted like a psycho hockey dad."

"Maybe I was a little over the top."

"Yeah, just a little. Now come back inside, sit quietly and enjoy what's left of the game?"

They go back inside the rink. By now, it's the third period and the Rebels are down 4-0. Near the end of the period, one of the Mississauga players is tripped and the team goes on the power play. Rick is about to stand and shout out some encouragement but the glare from Lois keeps him in his seat. The game ends at 4-0. The parents shuffle out of the rink and once again form little discussion groups in the lobby. The game is dissected and rehashed until players make their way out to pick up their parents for the drive home. Once out in the parking lot, Kyle looks up at his dad. "What was all the screaming about in the second period? Were you in a fight?"

"Yeah, there was a bit of an altercation. Hey, don't forget. Fighting is allowed in hockey."

CHAPTER 20

"I stand by all the misstatements that I've made."
Dan Quayle

Jerry and Margaret patiently await the arrival of the Minister for their weekly update meeting. The meetings provide Rick with progress reports on the consultation process and other issues that arise. Barbara brings in a pot of coffee for them while they wait for Rick to arrive. Margaret turns to Jerry. "So how do you want the consultation meetings to be run? What involvement will the Minister want to have?"

"I think we will provide him with a list of questions he should be asking each group. He may have some of his own. If you have a follow up question on anything raised during the exchange between the Minister and the presenters, then you can ask them at the end. As much as possible, we want him to appear as if he is running the show."

"That should be no problem. We've already drafted questions for him. However, he is known to shoot off his mouth. Some stakeholders are already agitated by the review. How do you propose we deal with a comment that might set someone off?"

"Pray the fire alarm goes off and the building is evacuated."

Just then Rick walks into the boardroom. "Good morning, everyone. Sorry I'm late. What's this about a fire evacuation?"

Jerry recovers quickly. "It's our plan for ending a meeting that gets too heated."

"Good thinking. Shall we get started?"

Margaret passes out some documents. "These are the consultation meetings for this week. We start off with the insurance industry, which is very eager to get in early. AIRS has written a note for each group outlining who it represents, who is attending, its key issues and some proposed questions for you to ask."

"This looks great. It will come in handy. Who is this group PAIN?"

"It's an acronym, which stands for People Against the Insurance Nightmare. It's a group of lawyers aligned with accident victims, most of whom are their clients."

He snickers. "Pain is a perfect name for lawyers since they are a collective pain in the butt."

Jerry jumps in. "Just a heads up. The group has a relationship to Christie Lefebre at the Sun. She has been known to write columns sympathetic to their position. So anything you say could potentially be in the paper the next morning."

"I'll be sure to keep my eyes open for any photographer that shows up for the meeting. What else do we have to talk about?"

Jerry edges forward in his seat. "Well, I do have one thing. The Canadian Council of Insurance Regulators or CCIR has a meeting at the end of the month in Regina. They are an inter-jurisdictional association of insurance regulators that get together to talk about common insurance issues. They would like to invite you to present on Ontario auto insurance reforms."

"Sounds fine to me. Can Lawrence draft a presentation for me?"

"Yes, he could."

"Good. Let them know I accept their invitation. If that's it, I'll see you both at the meeting."

The consultation meetings lead off with a discussion with the insurance industry. When Margaret and Jerry arrive for the meeting the next morning, the insurance industry representatives are already seated in the Minister's boardroom. Jerry recognizes Chip Bonham from the Insurance Association of Canada. The other people present are John Leifer, president of the Canadian division of American General Insurance and chair of the Association's board, and Steve Lamont, legal counsel to the Association. Steve has been with the Association for almost thirty years and has been down this road on many occasions. His white hair and wrinkled face make him look dour and cantankerous. They are still doing introductions when Rick struts into the boardroom. "Good morning everyone and thanks for coming. I see everyone has been doing introductions so let's get started. As you all know, I've been entrusted by the government to deliver a twenty-five percent rate reduction for drivers in the province. I've set up a series of meetings with interested parties to solicit advice before the government acts to bring down rates. I'm interested in your views on how we might accomplish this. So I'm going to turn the floor over to you, gentlemen."

Chip Bonham begins the presentation. "Thank you Minister. The insurance industry believes that consumers deserve a competitive auto insurance system that delivers affordable premiums for all drivers and fair benefits for injured accident victims. This can only be achieved with a commitment to real reforms that address costs. Reducing auto insurance rates without a plan to tackle the root problems in the auto insurance system will have a negative impact on drivers, insurers and, ultimately,

Ontario's economy. Since premiums are tied to claims costs, we are advising you to consider measures that help reduce claims costs. No magic wand will make costs disappear."

"Look, you people know I have an insurance background. I've been dealing with insurers for a long time. I speak to my clients every day and their view of the claims process is not positive. Insurers are well known for having short arms and deep pockets. If you think I am going to buy into your scorch the earth plan to slash benefits down to nothing, then you people are smoking some strange tobacco."

"Minister, if you understand insurance," John Leifer almost has a scolding tone. "Then you realize that there is a direct correlation between the cost of insurance claims and the premiums we need to charge."

"Yes I do. I also know that overhead and administrative costs are part of the formula. So are profits. I expect the companies to do their part to help the government meet its policy objective." He slams his fist on the table to emphasize the point.

Jerry is in a bit of shock although by now he should be getting accustomed to the outbursts. The Deputy Minister jumps in. "I think what the Minister is trying to say is that the government is looking for a balanced approach. Everyone is going to have to feel some pain." Chip continues with his presentation, which predominantly deals with the industry's perspective of costs in the system. After a few questions from Rick, the meeting wraps up. The men in the expensive suits slink out, not looking too happy.

As soon as they walk out, Rick turns to the group with a big grin. "That was a lot of fun. Bring on the next group!" He notices a young man in a dark suit at the end of the table who has remained after the insurance industry representatives leave. He had been writing away throughout the meeting with the insurers.

"Who are you?"

The Deputy Minister responds. "This is Dan Keith who works for me in the Secretariat. Dan will be taking notes at all the consultation meetings for us."

"Yeah, that's a good idea. For a minute, I thought he was planted here by the IAC." He begins to laugh at the thought. "Welcome Dan." Dan looks up and smiles.

The next group to present is the Ontario Massage Therapist Association. The two representatives, Leslie Burns and Kevin Sutherland, introduce themselves. Both are in their early thirties and eager to promote their profession. Massage therapy lacks the image of some of the other health professions. Rick does the identical introductory remarks and invites Leslie, who is the association's executive director, to begin her presentation. "I would like to thank you for the opportunity to present to you on such an important issue. The Ontario Massage Therapist Association, as the professional association of registered massage therapists in Ontario, provides support, professional development and networking opportunities for its 1,200 members, as well as a referral and information service to the public. The practice of massage therapy is the assessment of soft tissue and joints of the body and the treatment and prevention of physical dysfunction and pain of the soft tissues and joints by manipulation to develop, maintain, rehabilitate or augment physical function, or relieve pain. Today, I'd like to address one issue and one issue only – the role of registered massage therapists in the auto insurance system."

"You have to excuse my ignorance. I've known people who go to chiropractors and massage therapists and masseuses – you know, body rubbers. Could you explain to me how the different categories are defined? Because you're talking about manipulating bones, rubbing and muscle relaxation, and these are three different areas. I'm not very familiar with massage therapists."

Leslie Burns' face takes on a lovely shade of crimson. Margaret jumps in to try and redirect the discussion. "Thank you Leslie, the government is well aware of the important role that massage therapists play in the healthcare sector, as well as part of the auto insurance system."

"I would like to respond to the Minister's question. You mentioned chiropractic first of all: their main scope of practice is to work with the joints of the body. They're well trained with soft tissues as well, but they usually defer to either physiotherapists or massage therapists. As for body rubbers, as you refer to them, they are not regulated health professionals. I'm not very familiar with the profession and even calling them professionals may be suspect."

"Well, the purpose of the consultation process and our meeting today is about bringing down the cost of insurance for Ontario drivers. I'm interested in hearing your ideas."

"Minister we are health professionals and not experts in insurance. We don't possess any special insight into how to lower auto insurance premiums. We are here to represent our members and our profession. Our clients benefit from our treatment and hope we don't become a casualty of some cost cutting exercise." Jerry notices that Rick quickly becomes bored. He has no interest in hearing about massage therapy. His focus is limited to auto insurance costs. There is little discussion after Leslie reaches the end of her presentation and the meeting ends early.

Following the massage therapists, there is an accident victim in a wheelchair that has asked to present to the Minister. Rick gets up to greet her and find a spot at the table for her. "Thank you for coming to speak to us today. I appreciate that you would want to share your story with me. So, why don't you go ahead and start."

"Thank you. My name is Renee Thames and I was rear-ended by a truck in 2007. I sustained serious and debilitating injuries that have me confined to a wheelchair. My insurance company, instead of helping me recover and supporting me, has fought me every step of the way..."

"Excuse me, Ms. Thames," Rick interrupts. "That must have been quite the collision to cause a spinal cord injury."

"I don't have a spinal cord injury."

"So what type of an injury has you in a wheelchair all this time?"

"I have fibromyalgia."

"Fibromyalgia? What's that?"

"It's a pain disorder associated with severe fatigue and sleep disturbances."

Rick looks around the room but no one shows any reaction. "So why are you in a wheelchair?"

"My limbs are too weak and painful to walk so I need the wheelchair to get around."

"So, let me see if I have this straight. Five years ago, you are rear-ended and develop some whiplash. All these years later, you're too tired and sore to be able to walk?"

"Fibromyalgia is a valid and complex disorder. It is recognized by rheumatologists and neurologists. But my insurance company has refused to. Instead, they send me to an endless string of medical hacks who either tell me it's in my head or I am a fake."

"I don't blame your insurance company. Who would believe that a rear-end collision could put you in a wheelchair?"

"I have been through hell. I got addicted to pain medication and then had to get detoxed. I had to fund my own therapy because my insurer cut me off. Isn't that what insurance is for?"

Margaret feels uneasy about where the discussion is going. The presenter is clearly getting upset. "Ms. Thames, we are not here to question the validity of your insurance claim. Our role is to provide a more efficient way to deliver auto insurance services. We thank you for sharing your experience with us. We wish you well in resolving your differences with your company."

The rest of the meeting goes without incident although stakeholders still appear to be in shock when they leave the boardroom. Jerry sighs quietly and stares at his pile of notes in front of him. He realizes the process is going to be even more painful than he had originally anticipated.

CHAPTER 21

**"Always do sober what you said you'd do drunk.
That will teach you to keep your mouth shut."
Ernest Hemingway**

Rick looks out the window of the Air Canada plane as it prepares for takeoff from Pearson International. The trip to Regina will take about three hours and twenty minutes, which Rick decides is a perfect opportunity to catch up on some sleep. He is quite pleased to get a break from the monotonous stream of whining stakeholders. Initially, he had thought the process would be engaging but it has quickly become annoying. Despite the government's mandate to lower auto insurance premiums, the groups coming in have their own agendas, from stiffer penalties for drunk drivers to better access to rehabilitation for the brain injured. As the nose of the Embraer 190 pulls up, Rick closes his eyes and tries to drift off. He knows he should be going over his presentation to CCIR members but he isn't meeting with them until tomorrow so there is plenty of time to get ready. The cabin noises begin to fade away and all he is conscious of is the steady drone of the jet engines. Soon he is not even aware of that noise.

The next thing Rick is aware of is feeling the plane begin its descent. When he opens his eyes, he notices it's still daylight in the Saskatchewan capital. He can make out rooftops with snow, which appear closer as the plane nears the airport. Just over an hour later, he is in a taxi heading to the Radisson Plaza Hotel. Rick has arranged to meet David Tusk, the Superintendent of the Financial Services Commission of Ontario, for dinner. Several hours later, the two are in the hotel's dining room having drinks and looking over the menu.

"Rick, what do you think you're going to have?"

"We're out west so I'm having a good old-fashion strip loin steak."

"So if the meeting was in Nova Scotia, you would have fish?"

"No, I hate fish," he says laughing. "I would still have a steak. What are you having?"

"I have to cut back on my red meat. The cholesterol thing. So I'm going to have the roast cornish hen."

"The mini-chickens. You must be on a diet. Well, knock yourself silly."

After their server takes their orders the Superintendent turns to Rick. "I thought I would give you a rundown on the CCIR members and what to expect."

"Thank you. Tell me what I should know about this bunch."

"The east coast insurance superintendents are always interested in what is going on in Ontario. However, the provinces with government-run insurance - Quebec, Manitoba, Saskatchewan and British Columbia - are likely to be less engaged during the discussion."

"This doesn't sound like too difficult compared to some of the stakeholder meetings I've had."

"You have to remember, the members see themselves as insurance experts so they have their own perspective on the delivery of auto insurance benefits. Some are going to throw in their two cents."

"Fair enough."

The rest of the evening is spent chatting about family, hockey and how cold it is in Regina. At the end of the evening, they say goodnight and head up to their separate rooms for the night.

In the morning, Rick orders room service for breakfast and reviews his notes for the presentation. He is scheduled to present at 9:30 a.m. and heads down a few minutes early. The meeting is being held in a small conference room in the lower level of the hotel. He waits outside until he is ushered in by CCIR support staff. The provincial regulators are sitting around large banquet tables, forming a large square. Rick is seated at one end and runs through his presentation, which takes about twenty-five minutes. The presentation covers the Ontario government's policy agenda and the process to achieve it. When he comes to the end of his presentation, Rick invites questions and comments.

Pat Gracey, the Nova Scotia Superintendent of Insurance, who is also the chair of CCIR, is the first to respond. "Thank you, Minister Tompkins, for coming to meet with us this morning. I understand from your presentation that the process for identifying premium reductions is well underway. Can you provide us with some insight on where you believe your government will find such significant savings?"

"I'm unable to at the moment. We are still in the process of consulting with our stakeholders."

The Alberta Deputy Minister of Finance jumps in. "Surely you had an idea of what direction your reforms were going to go when you announced that you would be tackling high premiums."

"Yes. We know we want to lower auto insurance premiums by twenty-five percent."

"But you must have had a rough plan on how to accomplish it."

"There was no plan. But we did set a target, which we are determined to meet."

A few snickers spread around the room. The British Columbia Superintendent of Insurance has an annoyed look on his face. "I'm a little shocked. The Ontario auto insurance system represents twenty-five percent of the property and casualty market in all of Canada. An initiative is underway to make significant changes that could potentially destabilize the Canadian insurance market but no one knows what they will look like."

The Ontario Superintendent comes to the defense of his Minister. "We are in the early stages of the reform process. I assure you that a great deal of deliberation will take place before changes are made. I am sure the Minister would be happy to return in the future, when he has more detailed information."

Rick is a little dejected as he looks around the room. "Yes, of course."

After some further discussion, the group moves on to its next agenda item and Rick returns to his room. There are a few hours until his flight back to Toronto and he decides to pack up his things. After checking out of his hotel, he takes a cab to the airport. It has been snowing all morning and the snow is beginning to accumulate. On the highway, traffic is mostly traveling in the left lane because the right lane has become largely snow covered. When Rick arrives at the Air Canada check-in counter, he learns that his 1:10 p.m. flight to Toronto has been delayed. He decides that may work out well since he can now squeeze in lunch before taking off.

Rick finds a seat at the bar in the GateWay Lounge and orders a sandwich and beer. Sitting next to him is a man who appears to be in his early fifties, wearing a dark suit and holding an overcoat in his lap. The man smiles when they make eye contact. "Where are you heading to?"

"Toronto but my flight is delayed. What about you?"

"I'm heading in the opposite direction – Vancouver. My flight is also delayed. I sometimes wonder if any flight ever leaves on time."

"Yeah, flying isn't what it used to be. It's such a hassle now."

"By the way, I'm Sean."

"Nice to meet you. I'm Rick. What do you do?"

"I'm in sales. I sell car parts. What about you?"

"I'm a Cabinet Minister in Ontario. But before getting elected, I was selling insurance."

"No shit. What are you drinking there, Minister Rick?"

"Just some draft beer."

"I hope you're a scotch drinker, as well."

"Yeah, I don't mind a shot of scotch once in awhile."

"Well, I see they have some twelve year old scotch behind the bar. Would you care to join me for a drink? It seems we both have some time to kill."

"I think I can manage that."

Sean signals for one of the bartenders to come over. "I see you have a bottle of Johnnie Walker Black Label scotch sitting there on your bar. How about pouring my friend and I a couple of shots?" The bartender grabs the bottle and pours them each a shot. Sean grabs his glass and holds it in the air. "Here's to good company at airport bars."

"Cheers." Rick takes a sip of the whiskey.

"Rick, you look like just a regular guy. How did you get mixed up in politics?"

"To be honest, I was never interested in politics. I ran in the last election as a favour to an old friend and never expected to get elected. Sort of fell into a new career. I feel a little like a fish out of water."

"Rick, politics is just another sales job. Except instead of selling insurance or car parts, you're selling bullshit."

"You got that right." Rick looks again at the departures board which is mounted on a wall in the bar. "It looks like my flight is pushed back another hour. Do you have time for another round?"

"I think they just posted 'To Be Determined' as the departure time for my flight. Another round would suit me fine."

Another thirty minutes pass by and the flights are pushed back further. Rick signals to the bartender and points to their glasses. "Another round here when you get the chance." Moments later, the bartender brings the bottle over and refills their glasses. They clink glasses again but this time throw back their drinks. Rick feels the warmth of the alcohol spread through his body.

They continue to chat and order some munchies to go with the booze. Then some more booze to go with the munchies.

Rick leans over to his new friend. "I have a confession to make."

"What's that?"

Rick is feeling somewhat relaxed from the alcohol. "I'm leading this big project for the government but I don't have a friggin' clue what I'm doing. Shhhh."

Sean lets out a big laugh. "That's all right. Probably nobody in government has a clue, either. Remember man, you're a salesman! Rick, you're falling behind: you Easterners ain't much good at drinkin'."

"My drinking is fine. You Westerners can't count too good." Rick is suddenly aware of the public address system announcing – *final boarding for Air Canada flight 1152 for Toronto departing from gate 14.* "Whoa Sean, that's my flight. I gotta get moving. Great spending the afternoon with you."

"Good meeting you too. Good luck getting home."

Rick begins a half sprint to his gate. The terminal begins

to slowly spin on him. A traveler pulling a suitcase suddenly appears in front of him. He can't avoid them and trips over the suitcase, tumbling onto his hands and knees. He pulls himself back up on his feet and continues to rush to the gate. By the time he reaches gate 14, he is red-faced and sweating. His shirt is half hanging out of his pants and his tie is over to one side. Rick pulls out his boarding pass and hands it to the attendant.

The attendant looks at him suspiciously. "Sir, have you been drinking?"

"As a matter of fact, I did make a stop at a lounge while I waited several hours for this flight to take off. Is that a problem?"

"Well, it might be. How much did you have to drink?"

"Frankly, I haven't been counting but I can assure you that I'm perfectly fine."

"Mr. Tompkins, you appear to be visibly intoxicated. For public safety reasons, Air Canada has a policy that denies intoxicated passengers the right to board one of its planes."

"Wait a minute, are you accusing me of being shitfaced?"

"Mr. Tompkins, please do not raise your voice. I will call one of our security personnel who will sit down with you to go over the policy."

"I don't need a briefing from you people. I need to get on that plane over there."

"I'm sorry that won't be possible, in the condition you're in."

A small little scrum of airport passengers and employees forms around the gate entrance. Some have pulled out their phones to record the confrontation. "I have been waiting all day to get on this friggin' plane and there is no way you are keeping me off!"

Two security officers appear. Both exhibit a demeanor somewhere between stern and nasty. One officer approaches Rick and places his hand on his upper arm. His grip feels more mechanical than human. "Sir, we would like to speak to you in private."

Rick decides this is about the right time to fold his cards and count his losses. "Umm, sure we can have a chat."

They escort Rick to a ten by ten barren room with a small desk and two chairs. One officer sits behind the desk, while the other stands by the door. The officer behind the desk pulls out a notepad. "Have a seat." Rick passively complies. "What is your name, sir?"

"Is this really necessary?"

"Yes, sir it is. Your name."

"Rick Tompkins."

"Can you provide me your boarding pass and some identification?"

Rick hands over his driver's license along with his now worthless boarding pass. The officer is busy writing away in his note pad. "How many alcoholic beverages did you consume today, Mr. Tompkins?"

"I'm not really sure. Look, I headed into a lounge waiting for my flight and struck up a conversation with someone. We shared a few drinks to pass the time. What's wrong with that?"

"What would you estimate to be the number of alcoholic beverages that you consumed today?"

"I don't know. Maybe six."

"Mr. Tompkins, you could be charged with public intoxication among other things. We are going to let you go this time. I advise you to sober up before attempting to board another flight."

"Thank you." Dejected and embarrassed, he leaves the office. He decides to stay overnight in Regina and book another flight in the morning. He also needs to come up with an explanation for Lois.

CHAPTER 22

**"Everything is funny as long as it is
happening to somebody else."
Will Rogers**

Lawrence likes to remind people how popular social media
has become. He often tells people that there are 50,000 YouTube
videos being viewed every second and sixty-five hours of video
uploaded every minute. He also tells people that just about
everyone is eventually going to be caught in an embarrassing
video. So it comes as no surprise, when doing his regular Google
searches on Sunday morning, that he comes across a YouTube
video featuring Rick Tompkins. Then he discovers a second
one. And a third one. Each one is shot from a different phone
but contains the same incident. In the videos, Rick is arguing
with an Air Canada gate attendant. He looks like a mess, with
a red, sweaty face and disheveled clothes. And he looks drunk.
Lawrence turns up the volume enough to hear the gate attendant
informing Rick that he appears to be too intoxicated to board a
plane. The first video just has 102 views, the next one has 405 but
the third has 17,477 views.

He grabs his phone and dials Jerry's number. "Jerry, I'm
sending you three links to YouTube videos that you need to see
pronto."

"Okay. What are they about?"

"Did the Minister mention anything out of the ordinary that might have occurred while he was in Regina?"

"No, but when it involves the Minister, ordinary rarely happens. I just got messages and links...oh, for Christ's sakes! Where did this shit come from?"

"My guess it that they are mobile uploads by people standing around that departure gate."

"Oh my god! This is not good. He looks hammered."

"Yup. If you listen closely you can make out the other person in the video. He appears to be telling Rick that he can't board the plane because he is drunk."

"He never mentioned a word of this. What an asshole!"

"That's because he probably never expected to be featured on social media. The videos were posted two days ago. The good news is that two videos have very few views between them. But the third one appears to be trending and is almost at 20,000 views already, which is not good."

"Well, maybe nobody knows who it is."

"Are you kidding? How do you think I found these? He's identified and the videos turned up on Google searches using his name. If you scroll down to the comments posted, you will notice that they aren't exactly complimentary. Let's see. This one calls him a loser. This one calls him a douche bag. A pathetic piece of crap. What idiots voted for this guy?"

"Okay, I've heard enough. How do we get these things taken down?"

"Only the person who posted the video can bring it down. You know, the funny thing is that most politicians get caught in an embarrassing situation on one YouTube video. Our guy has outdone them all and has three videos."

"What can I say? He's an overachiever. I'm going to make Cabinet Office and the Premier's Office aware of the video. Let's hope the mainstream media and the Opposition parties don't find this."

"Well, let me know how I can help."

"Will do." Jerry hangs up and begins dialing the one person in this world whom he least wants to break bad news to: Geneva Horvath. "Hey Geneva, it's Jerry."

"I'm in a bit of a hurry, Switzer. What is it?"

"We have a bit of a situation that you need to be aware of. It seems Minister Tompkins' uneventful trip to Regina last week was not so uneventful. There was a bit of an incident which found its way onto YouTube."

"What are you talking about?"

"He was booted off a plane for being intoxicated. I've just forwarded a link to a video to you."

After a bit of a pause, she finally responds. "WHAT... THE...FUCK!"

"By the way, there are three such videos. He had a bit of an audience."

"Who did he meet with, Norm and Cliff from Cheers?"

"I will get all the details of what happened. I just wanted to give you a heads up in case this goes viral."

"It's already viral. While we've been chatting, the number of views has increased by several hundred."

Jerry's next call is to Rick. "Hi Rick."

"Hey Jerry. What's up?"

"Rick did anything out of the ordinary happen this past week in Regina?"

"Nothing I can recall. Why?"

"Really. Nothing comes to mind? I ask because you are featured in several YouTube videos getting booted off a plane in Regina for being hammered. Some people might consider that out of the ordinary. But perhaps you get booted off planes on a regular basis so it's no big deal."

Rick sighs. "My flight was delayed by a couple of hours. I headed to a lounge to kill some time, grab a bite and have a beer. I met some guy from B.C. and ended up having a few more drinks. The next thing I know, I'm being turned away at the gate by some uptight jerk. How the hell did it get on YouTube?"

"People like to record embarrassing moments when it involves a Cabinet Minister and then post them online. Have you not noticed that when you are out in public, people have their phones out? They're not just making phone calls."

"Yeah, I get it. So what do we do now?"

"I've been in contact with the Premier's Office already. The problem is we don't know how widespread this will get. There is no way to predict what becomes viral on the Internet. I'll get back to you." Jerry's phone vibrates to indicate he has an incoming call. "I've got another call. I'll speak to you later."

"Hi Lawrence, what have you got."

"The video is on the *Toronto Sun* website with a heading *Drunk Minister Booted From Flight*. I think we can officially say this has gone viral."

"Wonderful. Thanks for the update. Don't answer any media calls yet. We are going to get bludgeoned in Question Period tomorrow morning."

Another call comes in on his phone. "Hello Geneva. What's up?"

"Head over to the Cabinet Office boardroom in Whitney Block at three this afternoon. You do realize that the Homer Simpson of Ontario politics may be out of a job over this, right?"

"Excuse me for not breaking into tears. I'll be there."

When Jerry gets to Whitney Block, he quickly clears the security detail at the front entrance and briskly heads to the elevators. Once he arrives at the sixth floor, he walks down the long corridor that leads to Cabinet Office. The receptionist directs him to the boardroom where the meeting is already in progress. In addition to Geneva, the Principal Secretary of Cabinet and Cabinet Office staff are seated around the table. They pause when he enters the room and he sits down in a vacant seat. Geneva is chairing the meeting, which he finds a little surprising.

She turns to Jerry. "Jerry, I think you know everyone. We have been discussing how to manage the damage from Tompkins' video. There are a limited number of options on how we can respond. We can fire him and this thing dies down very quickly. I would love for that to happen. However, it sets a precedent for the future when other ministers might be guilty of unflattering behavior. The Premier does not want to open that door. He feels it is too early in the mandate to provide the Opposition with a Minister's "scalp" to parade in front of the public. He feels we are on 'safe ground' on this one because it doesn't involve a breach of trust or corruption. But we do have a Minister who we may want to demote from Cabinet at some time in the future."

"The other option, of course, would be to hold our ground and claim that this doesn't merit dumping someone from Cabinet. It means this drags on for days or longer. But eventually the public will become bored with this. I mean how many times can you watch the same video? However, this doesn't necessarily play well on Main Street. The Premier would like to hang on to the Minister, if possible. It really depends on how much fallout there is. We expect the Opposition to demand that the Minister be fired. The Premier feels it would be a sign of weakness to let him go. Cabinet Office will be preparing some messaging for Question Period this week. Any questions?"

Jerry provides a weak acknowledgement. "None from me."

As the boardroom empties out, Geneva pulls Jerry aside. "It

would be good if we could make some positive announcement in regards to auto insurance reforms. It would divert some attention away from this other nonsense."

"I'll talk to the Deputy Minister and see if we can come up with something. Let's catch up in the morning, before Question Period."

CHAPTER 23

"If you can't dazzle them with brilliance, baffle them with bull." W.C. Fields

Rick pulls up in front of the new Castlemore Community Centre, just minutes before the start of the opening day ribbon-cutting ceremony. He has been invited as a special guest speaker. Ameena 3 and Lawrence have accompanied Rick to deal with media requests and constituents. As Rick parks the car, Lawrence notices several reporters loitering in front of the entrance. "Hang on. We got media waiting for us."

Rick turns to Lawrence. "Don't worry. I can handle them."

"That's what I'm afraid of. You realize they are going to be asking about the YouTube video? What do you plan on saying?"

"Nothing. I'm going to tell them I'm late for the ceremony but will answer the questions once I'm done inside. Meanwhile, the two of you will be working out what I should say."

"Great idea, Boss!" Ameena 3 is relieved to hear that they will have some time to pull something together rather than having to come up with some messaging on the spot, while sitting in the car.

"Okay, let's do it." With that, Rick bounds out of the car with his staff running to keep up. When the pack of reporters spot them, they are immediately drawn to Rick as if pulled by an invisible magnetic force. All the while, they are shouting out questions.

"Minister, can you tell us about the incident at the Regina airport?"

"Are you drunk in the video posted on YouTube?"

"Have you been asked to resign from Cabinet?"

"Minister, do you believe you have a drinking problem?"

Rick stops in front of the group and holds up his hands. "Hang on there, folks. I'm sorry but I'm late for the opening ceremonies and need to get inside. I'll be done in about thirty minutes, at which time I will be happy to meet you back here to answer all your questions." With that, he steps around the reporters and walks into the building, followed by his staff.

As they step into the lobby, an anxious looking woman approaches them. "Minister Tompkins, I'm Angela Stamos, director of city facilities. I'm so glad that you could join us this afternoon."

"It's my pleasure. I've brought some of my staff with me. This is Lawrence, my communications coordinator, and this is Ameena 3, who runs my constituency office. I believe you've been working out the arrangements for today with Ameena 3."

"Yes. It's always nice to put a face with the voice and also nice to meet you, Lawrence. Now why don't you follow me to the auditorium because we are just about ready to start."

She leads them into a large multi-purpose room. On one side are tables set up with coffee, tea and cookies. There is a small crowd standing in front of the table, scarfing down the free goodies. Most of the people in the room are already seated on stacking chairs, facing the front of the room. There are about 200 chairs set up and almost half of them are filled. Lawrence and Ameena 3 find two seats in the back to work on some speaking points for Rick without disturbing people listening to the speeches.

Angela takes Rick to the front of the room where there is a riser set up with some seats for the dignitaries and a podium. Also attending is the Brampton Deputy Mayor, the City Councillor for the area and two Regional Councillors. Rick shakes hands with the others and takes a seat. He notices that none of the reporters at the front of the building have bothered to come inside.

When the ceremonies come to a conclusion, Lawrence and Ameena 3 quickly make their way to the front to meet with Rick. He is chatting with one of the councillors and notices Lawrence is signaling for him to come over. He excuses himself and walks over the two anxious employees. "What have you got?"

"We have some basic messaging for you. We just need a few minutes to go over it before stepping outside."

"Sure thing. Hang on a second." He spots Angela and calls her over. "Where do these exits lead to?" He points to a set of doors in the corner.

"Thank you again for doing this, Rick. Those doors lead to the parking lot."

"I can get to my car through those doors?"

"Yes, you can."

"People, follow me." Rick puts his coat on and heads to the doors. Lawrence and Ameena 3 run to the back of the auditorium for their coats then scramble to catch up. As they head outside, they see Rick running to his car.

Ameena 3 turns to her colleague. "Holy shit, we better hustle or he'll be leaving us behind." They pick up their pace and find themselves running to the car as well. As they approach Rick's car, the assembly of reporters notices the three of them running and give chase. Lawrence has a fair amount of foot speed and nearly catches Rick. Rick gets to the car first and jumps into the driver's seat and slams the car into drive. Just then, Lawrence reaches the car and hops in the back. Rick then pulls the car up to an exhausted Ameena 3, who dives into the backseat.

Ameena 3 is face down in the backseat, trying to catch her breathe. "Oh my god...I can barely breath!"

Lawrence is coughing from breathing in the dry wintry air. "Minister...are you...out of your mind?"

"Relax guys. I really didn't want to talk to the media. But thanks for the speaking notes," chuckles Rick.

The media scrum looks on from the parking lot, a little annoyed and dejected. They turn to go back to their cars when one reporter suddenly joins them. "Hey guys! I just got a great video of the Minister sneaking out the backdoor and running to his car. This is going to be a big hit on YouTube."

———

Jerry sits on his living room sofa, absent-mindedly rubbing the day-old stubble on his chin as he calls the Deputy Minister. "Good evening, Margaret. I'm terribly sorry to disturb you at home. The Minister has run into some trouble and we need some assistance."

"No problem. How can I help?"

"There are a number of YouTube videos of the Minister being turned away from an Air Canada flight last week. We have just been made aware of them today. We expect Question Period to be rocky tomorrow. The Premier's Office would like something favorable to announce to counter some of the negative attention this will bring. Do you have anything?"

"Oh my! How unfortunate for the Minister. I can't think of anything to announce off the top of my head. We are too early in the process to make any reform announcements."

"I'm desperate. Do we have anything old we can recycle?"

"When I get into the office tomorrow morning, I will discuss it with the staff and get back to you."

"Thanks a lot Margaret. Enjoy the rest of your evening." He tosses his phone onto the coffee table and, with an exasperated sigh, leans back until his head is on one of the arms of the sofa. Within seconds, the phone begins to chirp and he picks it up. "Hi Mom."

"Jerry, is everything alright?"

"Yeah, everything's fine. Why are you asking?"

"Your father and I feared that you had been forced to go underground and were in a witness protection program."

"What are you talking about?"

"Well it's been so long since we've heard from you that we thought maybe you were in some kind of trouble and were unable to reach us."

"Mom, that is so ridiculous. And it hasn't been that long. What's up with you guys?"

"I have a serious problem and need your help."

"What is it?"

"The TV remote isn't working properly and I haven't been able to record Dancing With The Stars. I'm pretty sure your father has done something to sabotage the remote. He hates that show and now I've missed the last two episodes."

"Mom, I left you instructions. What did you do with them?"

"I can't find them. I'm sure your father has thrown them out."

"I'm sure Dad hasn't been sabotaging your TV viewing. I'll drop by this week and walk you through the instructions again."

"You're such a sweet boy. I just don't understand why women aren't falling all over you. Your Uncle Bernie says you might be a homosexual. Umm, are you?"

"No Mom. I'm not a homosexual. I'll talk to you later. Bye."

He picks up his laptop off the coffee table and places it on his chest. He then pulls up the YouTube videos. There are now 33,445 views of the one video and a growing list of comments. Nothing like a political scandal to get people worked up. Perhaps Rick won't survive this. Jerry decides that wouldn't be such a bad thing. He shuts down his computer and calls it a day.

At 8:00 a.m. the next morning, Jerry and Lawrence meet in his office to go over the messaging from Cabinet Office. Jerry summarizes the strategy. "Here is the message we will be repeating: The Minister had some drinks during the time he was in the airport lounge but was not drunk."

"That's not what the video shows and what if reporters track down that gate attendant?"

"He may get his fifteen minutes of fame. We will say that he overreacted. It will come down to his word against that of the Minister."

There is a knock on the door. Jerry looks up and sees Margaret Bouton at the door. He signals for her to come in. "Good morning, Margaret. Have you got anything for us?"

"Good morning. I have something but I'm afraid it's not much. We recently created an online auto insurance shopping guide to help consumers find insurance. There was a media release two months ago announcing the guide. I'm sorry that's all I have."

"It will have to do."

She hands him a sheet of paper. "This is the media release that was issued."

"Thanks a lot. I'll share this with Cabinet Office." As the Deputy Minister leaves for her office, Jerry turns to Lawrence. "I have to rush this over to Cabinet Office and then I will meet you in the Legislative Building for Question Period."

"Okay. See you later."

After dropping off the media release to Cabinet Office, Jerry crosses Queen's Park Circle and enters the Legislative Building. By the time he arrives at the Chambers, the session has already started. Several visitors in the gallery are introduced - students from St. Luke's Catholic Elementary School, a few farmers representing the Dairy Farmers of Ontario, board members of the Canadian Cancer Society and individuals from CJPAC, the Canadian Jewish Political Affairs Committee.

The Speaker announces that it's time for Question Period. The first question comes from the Leader of the Opposition, Lawrence Shedden. "Mr. Speaker. My question is for the Premier. I am wondering if you are one of the 67,000 people who has watched a video of the Minister responsible for Auto Insurance Reform publicly intoxicated. If not, you should see this video. Frankly, I find the behavior that I observed on the video to be inappropriate for an Ontario Cabinet Minister and I'm sure most Ontarians would agree with me. Premier, will you hold the Minister responsible? Will you fire your Minister responsible for Auto Insurance Reform, apologize to the voters for this disgusting display of bad behavior and put a new Minister in place that we can have confidence in?"

The House breaks out with cheering from the Opposition side and jeering from the Government side. The Speaker warns several members that they will be ejected if they continue to disrupt the Legislature. The Premier rises to respond. "Mr. Speaker. I'm pleased to see that the Leader of the Opposition keeps up to date on members of the House through social media. The Minister responsible for Auto Insurance Reform was in Regina last week consulting with insurance regulators across the country. He was there to explore all possible avenues for bringing down scandalously high insurance rates for overburdened Ontario drivers. I would like to remind the Leader of the Opposition that when he was Premier, auto insurance rates rose by almost ten percent. I suggest that paying scandalously high insurance rates is what Ontarians really care about. I am committed to lowering auto insurance rates by twenty-five percent. No, I will not be firing the Minister. I want him to continue to deliver badly needed financial relief to Ontario drivers."

Cheering and jeering break out again, but this time from opposite sides of the House. Again, the Speaker attempts to bring back order. The Leader of the Opposition rises again. "I have a supplementary question. Premier, we have school children in the gallery and thousands at home following what goes on in the House. What type of message are you providing when you are condoning public drunkenness from your ministers? I ask you again today to dismiss the Minister. Show that you care."

The Premier rises again to respond. "I see the Leader of the Opposition considers himself to be judge, jury and executioner. As I have previously mentioned, the Minister was in Regina working on behalf of Ontarians. While waiting several hours for a delayed flight, he had lunch and several beverages. Unfortunately, he was the victim of an overzealous airline employee who made a judgment call that the Minister was intoxicated. The Minister was not intoxicated but I'm not here to criticize the gate attendant. He was concerned for public safety and made a decision, albeit without any real evidence. No, I do not condone public drunkenness. I also don't condone public lynching. I will not be firing the Minister."

Looking on, Jerry determines that the government may have weathered the storm for now. There are no more questions about the video. Several minutes later, a question is directed to the Minister responsible for Auto Insurance Reform from Daniel McClintock, a Conservative backbencher. This is the "soft lob" question to make the Minister look good. "My question is for the Minister responsible for Auto Insurance Reform. My constituents look forward to lower auto insurance rates in the near future. I do get frequent emails and calls about what drivers can do in the interim to save money on auto insurance. What can I tell my constituents?"

Rick has a grin on his face as he rises to answer the question. "Thank you for your question. It so happens that two months ago, the government created an online auto insurance shopping guide to assist consumers in finding the best rate. Many drivers aren't aware that there are significant differences in rates charged from company to company. Our online guide will help drivers find the best rates, and it also provides tips on how to tailor your coverage to save money. All drivers will benefit in a year from now when the government introduces reforms to save them money." Jerry rolls his eyes. He determines that will be it for auto insurance related questions and gets up to return to his office.

At the end of the day's session, reporters form scrums around ministers and MPPs for sound bites to be used for the evening news. *Toronto Sun* reporter Christie Lefebre is waiting for Rick to exit the Chambers. "Hello Minister, nice to see you again. Can I ask you a question about your trip to Regina?"

"I really have nothing to say."

"I've spoken to the gate attendant who confirms that you were quite drunk when he stopped you from boarding that plane. Do you have any comment to make?"

"I was perfectly fine. The gentleman was mistaken."

"Were you sober enough to be driving a car?"

"I was neither driving a car nor flying a plane that day. Your paper loves to make something out of nothing. I understand. You make money by selling papers. But I have nothing else to say." Rick quickly walks past her before she can ask any more questions, leaving her poised with recording device in hand, and a disappointed frown on her face.

CHAPTER 24

"Lawyers, I suppose, were children once."
Charles Lamb

Rick is driving down to Queen's Park from Brampton for another round of consultation meetings when his phone rings. "Hello Rick, it's Don Brand." When Don calls, he's usually strictly business.

"Good morning, Don. How are you and Sylvia?"

"We're fine. Rick, let me get straight to the point. I see that you are up to your neck in manure again. You seem to constantly find new ways to embarrass yourself and the family."

"I think you are getting a distorted view based on media reports."

"Really? Are you telling me that you didn't consume enough alcohol to get denied entry onto an airplane? Are you telling me the media made that all up?"

"Yes it happened but…"

"There are no buts. People are watching you and do you know what they see? A bumbling fool. You need to pull up your socks. Life only gives you so many chances."

"Yes sir," responds Rick but Don is already gone. Rick sighs. What a great way to start the day. An ass-kicking from Don Brand. Forty minutes later he has parked his car and is crossing the street after picking up a coffee from Tim Hortons. He turns to head into Ferguson Block when a voice calls out. "Can you spare some change?" It is a familiar vagrant who is usually located down the street closer to Queen's Park Circle. His two dogs are stretched out on the sidewalk beside him. He is holding a sign that reads: 'My EX-WIFE had a better lawyer.'

Rick has an annoyed look on his face. He snarls back, "Get a job!" One of the dogs begins to growl at Rick. The second dog joins in and begins to bark. Rick scampers into the building.

Several minutes later, he is sitting in his office preparing for the next consultation meeting with PAIN. The notes prepared by staff indicate that the group is pretty much dormant except when the government is considering auto insurance reforms. As far as he is concerned, these groups are like piranhas. They show up at the first sign of food, with voracious appetites. When he walks into his boardroom, it is already filled with staff and PAIN representatives. The PAIN people jump to their feet to introduce themselves. Rick does his standard introductory remarks and then invites the group to start their presentation.

"Thank you Minister Tompkins for agreeing to meet with us today. I'm Ben Siebert, the only lawyer in the group and I have been designated as the presenter for today. You likely know that People Against the Insurance Nightmare or PAIN has been around for a couple of decades. We are a coalition of innocent accident victims, health care professionals, business and labor representatives, police and lawyers. With the proposed reforms this government is contemplating, PAIN feels compelled to make representations to this government to stave off possible dramatic and draconian changes that will further erode the rights of the innocent accident victim in favor of the insurance company. In any insurance scheme, the government must try to balance the insurance premiums the consumer has to pay with the rights accruing to the accident victim, for benefits and damages."

Rick who has been on his BlackBerry throughout the presentation looks up with a bored expression on his face. "Thanks for that passionate presentation. So what recommendations do you have for me on how to save drivers twenty-five percent on their insurance?"

"We have no concrete suggestions. Our organization's mandate is not to protect the interests of insurance industry profits. We are here to plead our case that you not reduce accident benefits or the ability to sue. It would be unfair to have accident victims carry the burden of producing lower premiums and higher profits for insurance companies."

Rick begins to get annoyed. "This isn't a difficult concept. Premiums go to pay to fix cars, pay accident benefits and settle lawsuits. What's left over is a company's profit. Drivers in Ontario tell us they are paying too much and we are committed to lowering premiums. So if we don't touch accident benefits and the ability to sue, how are people going to be able to save money on their insurance? Cars need to be fixed and insurance companies need to make some profit."

"It isn't PAIN that is proposing such a large premium reduction and it's not our responsibility to come up with a solution. We are here to represent the interests of our constituents."

Seeing where this is leading, Margaret Bouton jumps in. "Thank you, Mr. Siebert, for bringing your perspective on the reforms to the group. We will certainly consider them as we move forward with this daunting task."

The meeting wraps up shortly after. Jerry who has been quiet throughout the meeting stays back after everyone has left to speak to Rick. "You know that you shouldn't be antagonizing the people coming in. They are concerned about possible changes and merely trying to get their message over to the government. You don't have to accept what they have to say but at least appear receptive."

"You mean kiss ass like Deputy Bow Wow? Not my style. We have spent weeks and weeks talking to people and no one has said anything helpful. This is a total waste of time."

"Perhaps your expectations are too high. The government is going to do what is necessary to accomplish its platform commitment. But part of the process is listening to people before it acts. The pain up front will reduce the pain down the road. As for the Deputy Minister, she is a thorough professional and doesn't deserve that off color label. Your success is very much tied to the work she and her team perform."

"Yeah, yeah. So, who are we up against this afternoon?"

"It's the Committee for Fair Auto Insurance." Rick cringes at the sound of the organization's name. "Let's try not to have the meeting break out into a brawl."

That afternoon, they reconvene in the Minister's boardroom to meet with the Committee for Fair Auto Insurance. The committee's chairperson gets up to greet Rick as he enters the room. "Good afternoon, Minister. Graham Wallace from Blidswell Morgan. Good to see you again and congratulations on the election results and your appointment."

"Thank you. Nice to see you again, as well. I know that our first meeting prior to the election was a little testy. I enjoy a good debate and want people to feel free to speak their minds." The comment causes Jerry's eyebrows to rise slightly.

"I completely agree, Minister. We are happy to exchange views even if we differ, which is why we are here today."

"Well, why don't you begin with your presentation? We are here to listen." Jerry is smiling now. He knows at least Rick is putting on a good show for the group.

"Thank you for the opportunity to meet with you and your staff. I would like to start off with an explanation of the role of lawyers in the auto insurance system. Lawyers often get demonized by the media, the public and certainly by insurance companies. Interestingly, the part that people forget is that insurers are also using lawyers to represent their interests. I know you previously referred to lawyers as robber barons and sharks. We take this as part of the hyperbole you get during an election campaign. Plaintiff lawyers help accident benefits recipients work their way through our complicated insurance legislation. We have clients with limited language skills and limited education. However, even educated clients cannot possibly understand the system well enough to represent themselves. We play an important role by creating balance in a system where the other side is well resourced. Lawyers advocate for accident victims, many of whom are quite vulnerable, facilitate their access to rehabilitation and reach settlements for clients so that they can go on with their lives. We are entitled to being compensated fairly for this work, which is no different than everyone else in the system."

Rick is smiling. No signs of any agitation. "Thank you, Graham, for putting things into perspective. Perhaps you can elaborate on your group's ideas regarding reforming the system. I would love to hear them."

"Yes, we have a number of ideas for the government to consider. Here are the main points. The remainder can be found in our submission. First, we would like to see better access to the courts for innocent accident victims. The current system has too many restrictions on the ability to sue an at-fault driver. This is fundamentally unfair. Second, we would like to see a streamlined accident benefits system with clear bundles of funding available for rehabilitation. Too much money is spent by insurers battling claims instead of paying them. The accident victims' health care providers know best what rehabilitation is needed. Insurers rely too heavily on insurance doctors who spend a few minutes examining a person that they really don't know. Too much money is being spent fighting small claims. Streamline the system and millions could be saved."

"Hmm. So that's your solution? Throw a lot more money at accident victims and that will save money? Kind of like letting drivers decide what speed to drive on the highway because they will always choose a safe speed, don't you think?"

"Minister, I don't think that is a fair analogy."

Jerry watches the forced smile disappear from Rick's face. "Maybe millions more can be saved by not having lawyers skim forty percent off of every dollar given to accident victims? Maybe then we would have more money to spend on accident victims and still provide premium reductions?"

"Minister, we think it is unfair and unproductive to lay the blame on lawyers. The Law Society of Upper Canada regulates legal fees and is of the view that what we charge is fair and appropriate."

"I was wrong to characterize lawyers as sharks. They are bloodsuckers! Sucking as many dollars out of the system as they can."

Jerry decides he can't sit back and listen anymore. "I know the Minister uses some strong language at times. We are open to all ideas on reforming the system. We will look at your ideas and have our actuarial consultants review your proposals to identify possible cost savings. Don't you agree, Minister?"

Rick glares at the collection of well-dressed lawyers at the other end of the table. "Yeah sure. Of course, we will have these marvelous ideas reviewed by our actuaries. I'm sure the savings will be quite impressive."

It is obvious that there is little benefit to be derived from continuing the meeting. It quickly winds down and the guests make a hasty exit. The staff exchange glances with each other. They say nothing but it's obvious to everyone that the consultation process is a complete bust. Soon they will be asked to begin developing options for reducing rates with not much to go on.

CHAPTER 25

"However beautiful the strategy, you should occasionally look at the results."
Winston Churchill

Rick is looking out his office window at the dreary scene outside. The dark grey clouds make if feel like the semidarkness associated with twilight. The mounds of snow left on the curbs by snow ploughs have long melted away, leaving a mixture of grey dirt and garbage, which is being dissolved and swept away by a spring rain. Rick checks the time and realizes he will be late for the meeting if he doesn't hustle. Jerry has called a half-day planning session with Secretariat staff to get a better grasp on where the government's reform agenda stands after four months of consultation, with every interest group and individual in the sector having had the ear of the Minister.

The meeting is being held in Macdonald Block, which is a two-story complex connected to four government office towers including the Ferguson Block, where Rick and the Secretariat are located. The planning session is being held in the Kenora Room, which is on the second floor, where all the meeting rooms are located. Rick arrives just as the meeting begins. The Deputy Minister distributes a thirty-page chart. "I'm passing around a chart that summarizes the position of all stakeholders based on submissions and presentations during the consultations. There is a lot of information here. But maybe we can start with the Minister's impression of the consultations. What areas would you like to see the reforms concentrate on? Where do you see cost savings based on what you have heard?"

"Well, I thought a lot of people were full of crap. Kind of disappointing. I didn't see much value for the time spent listening to these people. There are few ideas we can use to drive down rates, from my perspective."

Margaret Bouton nods in agreement. "Yes, that is typical of a consultation process. If you ask people to comment on a specific proposal or idea, they will. But if you keep it open-ended, they will use it to push their own personal agenda. So let's walk through what we heard. I'll turn it over to one of my staff. Go ahead, Merrell."

"Thank you. We heard many ways to enhance the system, including more no-fault benefits and better access to the courts. These suggestions may have their merit under another initiative but not one related to premium reduction."

Rick jumps in. "Yes, I agree. So what's left over?"

"One proposal involves reducing the profits of insurance companies. I will get into the feasibility of this proposal and all the others after running through the list. Introducing government-run auto insurance. Getting the Ministry of Health, through its health insurance program, OHIP, to cover the cost of all medical benefits. Introducing managed care, similar to what exists in the U.S. healthcare system. Abandoning no-fault and returning to a tort system. Cutting the level of accident benefits. That is your choice of options, though it could also be a combination of options, such as reducing insurer profitability and abandoning no-fault."

Rick is frowning. Jerry makes a suggestion: "Why don't we

discuss each approach in more detail and try to determine the feasibility of each?"

Merrell continues. "There are a lot of stakeholders and consumers who believe insurance companies make too much money. There is no question that companies are profitable. If they weren't, they wouldn't be here and we have seen companies withdrawing from the Ontario market. However, if you were to somehow introduce a cap on profits, it might change that trend. Keep in mind that over half of the insurance in the province is sold by foreign owned companies. If you limit how much they can earn, they might transfer the capital invested in Ontario, elsewhere. That could cause an insurance crisis in the province."

Rick leans back in his chair and responds. "I agree insurance companies are earning decent bucks here. I don't think profits are the problem. I believe competition for market share balances price and profit. Let's not go there."

"There were a number of stakeholders who advocated for a government-run system. They point to provinces like Quebec and Manitoba where the systems are much more generous but premiums paid by drivers are lower than in Ontario. The public systems are much more efficient. In Quebec, the administrative cost of operating the system is under ten percent of the premium while in Ontario, it's almost forty percent. Road safety initiatives are built into the insurance systems to keep the number of accidents and claims down."

The Deputy Minister jumps in. "We also realize that this government has no mandate to take over the auto insurance market nor does it have an interest in doing so. It's just an idea thrown out there that would allow the government to meet its commitment around lower rates."

Rick is nodding. "There is no f-ing way this government is looking at nationalizing auto insurance. Let's move on."

"The next idea involves having the government take over the medical portion of auto insurance through its health insurance program. We estimate that medical costs are close to twenty-five percent of auto premiums, which would go a long way towards meeting the government's commitment. However, there are some implications. Auto insurance covers medical costs not covered by OHIP, which would mean expanding coverage to what are now uninsured services and creating an obvious two-tiered health system. If you are injured at home you get one level of service but if you are in your car you get another, better level of service."

Rick is shaking his head. "This doesn't really lower the cost of auto insurance. You are just transferring the cost of insurance from drivers to taxpayers. But in reality, it's coming out of the same pocket. Okay, next."

"The next idea is managed care. For those not familiar with the concept, managed care plans are used by health insurers in the U.S. to keep cost down. Insurers have contracts with health care providers and medical facilities to provide care for plan members, at reduced costs. These providers make up the plan's network. When you need to access health care services, you are limited to providers within the network. If we were to adopt managed care in Ontario, auto insurers would contract with providers and rehabilitation facilities to provide services at lower costs. Policyholders would give up the right to choose where they go in exchange for lower premiums."

"Sounds interesting. What's the downside?"

Margaret responds to his question. "We question the ability of insurers to set up networks. It requires sophisticated procurement and quality assurance processes to maintain. This may drive smaller insurers right out of the marketplace. As well, in large cities like Toronto and London, there is an oversupply of health care providers but in smaller communities, there are shortages. Insurers will have no leverage with providers where they are the only game in town. This might make sense to a private health care insurer that is only purchasing health care services but health care is only one component of the services paid for by auto insurers. Considering all the costs and benefits, the amount of savings may not be significant."

"All right, let's move on to the next option."

Merrell gets to the bottom of her list. "What's left is cuts to no-fault benefits and abandoning no-fault altogether for a tort-based system where you can sue an at-fault driver for compensation. They are almost identical options since, to achieve a twenty-five percent premium reduction, you would need to pretty much eliminate no-fault and return to tort."

Jerry looks puzzled. "Isn't a tort system also expensive? I recall Ontario moved to no-fault to reduce the cost of auto insurance. So how can moving back to tort be cheaper?"

Margaret agrees. "Yes, you are correct. Ontario moved to no-fault in 1990 for what was believed, at the time, to be a cheaper product. Initially it was, but as the system matured, costs rose and constant reforms created a complex system to administer. Administering two systems – no-fault and tort – is expensive. Eliminating no-fault will transfer some costs over to tort but will remove the high cost of administering no-fault claims."

Rick leans back in his seat with his hands clenched behind his head. "Will this achieve our twenty-five percent savings for drivers?"

"We don't have accurate costing on many of these options and, to be honest, actuaries don't have the data to give precise projections. However, this option is not likely to generate much savings and it has its risks."

Rick begins to speak. "So I've been listening to you people all morning. What I'm getting from all this is that we have nothing but a bunch of crappy options." His face begins to flush and his voice rises. "Well folks, I've got news for you. This ain't good enough. We spent months on this stuff and you have come back to tell me you got a big pile of nothin'. I could have gotten the same out of a class of first year poli sci students."

Jerry tries to interject. "Margaret, I'm sure this is just your preliminary review of the options and a more extensive and detailed list is coming."

Margaret pushes back. "Let's be frank, here. The government has decided to reduce premiums by one-quarter. That is a significant number. You can't merely tinker with the system to create that much savings. You are talking about major systemic changes. You will have to abandon the system we have and introduce a brand new model, and not just any new model. It will have to be much cheaper."

"Folks, you are going to have to come up with something better. I'm giving you one month to produce a viable plan for this government or heads will roll. I think we're done here."

CHAPTER 26

*"O! for a muse of fire, that would ascend
the brightest heaven of invention."*
William Shakespeare

What Ever Happened To Muses?
Mort Blanger, National Post Columnist

She was once the female figure - deity, mistress, lover, wife and even platonic companion - whom poets, musicians and artists called upon for inspiration. For hundreds of years, in one form or another, the Muse was often essential to the creation of art.

Poets stopped using Muses long ago. Instead, they turned to caffeine, alcohol and amphetamines to boost their creativity. Painters and musicians abandoned Muses more recently. We now learn that having a Muse isn't restricted to artists.

But Muses have changed over time. For centuries, Muses were comfortable being subordinate to their artists, bound to his aesthetic and sexual needs, while the artist was free to live as he chose. Many modern Muses were powerful and creative women in their own right. For example, Salvador Dali's wife and Muse, Gala, shrewdly tortured her sex-averse husband with her many open affairs.

Nowadays, Muses are hard to find. There have been a few celebrated ones in recent years, including Yoko Ono who met John Lennon several years before The Beatles broke up. But the world of Muses has thinned out. Artists may still have a Muse, but the relationship has changed. These days a Muse is an equal partner and may have equal talent, which diminishes her function as an inspiration. In response, Muses appear to have broadened their appeal to other celebrities, including athletes and politicians. Athletes call them puck bunnies, cleat chasers and jersey chasers. In politics, they appear as interns, aides and assistants. As long as there are men seeking inspiration, there will likely always be Muses.

Rick is becoming somewhat disillusioned with the review process and the Secretariat. The Premier's Office wants to manage him like a trained seal. They have no respect for him, and as far as he is concerned, the feeling is mutual. Every speech he makes is scripted by others. He feels like he is under a microscope at the Cabinet table. The Premier's Office even screens the office staff that he hires, which makes him distrust his own staff.

He has discussed it with Lois, who is sympathetic but suggests he needs to get accustomed to the environment. Rick is beginning to feel very isolated in Queen's Park. There is no one he can trust or confide in, certainly no one in his office. Jerry is a backstabber and Rick is positive that he is reporting everything to Geneva, which is where his loyalties really lie. Lawrence is beginning to get on his nerves. Rick is convinced he is an airhead who has no opinion of his own. He just tells you what he thinks you want to hear. And then there is Margaret Bouton. She is a know-it-all and is always trying to show him up.

The thought of having to drop into the office today depresses him. He has considered trying to hire his own advisor but he is maxed out on his staffing budget. Maybe he needs to take a slightly different approach to his situation. He could come up with an informal unpaid arrangement that wouldn't have to show up on the books. A recent column in the *National Post* entitled *"What Ever Happened To Muses?"* has piqued his interest. Rick has always been attracted to the idea of a Muse - a woman who is the source of inspiration for a creative artist. But why does it have to be an artist? He considers himself to be a creative person, although he doesn't necessarily express his creativity through artistic endeavors.

The *Post* columnist laments the declining status of Muses. However, he also suggests that female inspiration is no longer limited to artists and can include other endeavors, including politics. Maybe that's what he is missing. A confidante who can inspire and guide him and would never betray him. An advisor with no personal ambition, someone who is there solely to serve him. What a difference that could make in his life! Rick recently sold a set of old golf clubs on Craigslist, so why not use Craigslist to locate a Muse?

Rick sits down at his computer and begins to check out the different Craigslist categories. He quickly narrows down the most appropriate categories to be: Jobs, Gigs and Personals. As he flips through the Jobs and Gigs categories, he quickly determines that these sections are related to paid positions and he isn't planning on paying this person. After all, a Muse should be adequately rewarded with the knowledge that she is inspiring him to greater accomplishments. Rick focuses on the Personals section and begins browsing through the different subcategories. It is obvious Rants and Raves is not appropriate. He finds Missed Connections amusing but not the right fit. The Casual

Encounters and Men Seeking Women categories are obviously intended for men interesting in dating and sex. He eventually decides that the Strictly Platonic section is the best fit.

He begins to craft his ad and, after about twenty minutes, is satisfied that he has the right wording. He posts it on the site. Responses will go to his anonymous Hotmail account, TrickyDicky.

I would really like to have a Muse - m4w

I've thought about having a muse - someone with an artistic flair who could inspire me, perhaps someone who is a free-spirit. Andy Warhol used to have a telephone friend that he never met. As the story goes, they'd chat most nights when both in their own homes and they actually never even met each other.

They'd simply be there for the other as a confidante to listen, chat, provide guidance and be his Muse. Just a someone on the other line happy to be the giver and taker of each other's mundane lives.

I'd like an online friend, a Muse, of exactly such a manner. We likely will never meet, so I don't care if you're gorgeous - though I'd prefer you to be interesting and intelligent.

He shuts down his computer and leaves for a meeting of the Priorities and Planning Committee of Cabinet. It's a mild spring day so instead of taking the tunnel to the Legislative Building, Rick decides to walk outdoors. The tulips are in full bloom in the flower beds around the Legislature. Squirrels are once again scampering around the grounds, looking for food. He keeps pulling out his BlackBerry to check for responses to his ad.

The Priorities and Planning Committee meetings are always held in the Cabinet boardroom on the second floor of the Legislative Building, just off of the Premier's office. The hallway outside the Premier's office is lined with portraits of past Ontario premiers. When Rick arrives, he enters through the anteroom, where lunch is still being set up. He walks into the Cabinet boardroom and sits down in the seat in front of his name card. Cabinet Office staff always distribute meeting material and name cards prior to each meeting. The name cards seem unnecessary to Rick since they all know each other. He understands it is more about seating arrangements. The Premier always sits in the middle of the table and the same ministers always sit next to him. Only ministers and the Secretary of Cabinet sit at the table. All others attending sit in chairs lining the walls of the room. Wood paneling covers half the walls with art works above the paneling. A landscape portrait called Autumn Rustling Leaves by Bev Rodin dominates the room.

Rick opens up his binder to review the meeting material. The agenda is dominated by policy initiatives that are to be included in the Spring Budget Statement, to be delivered by the Finance Minister. Rick expects the meeting to be exceptionally dull. The Premier has just shown up, setting the meeting in motion. Rick gets up to grab a sandwich from the anteroom. About thirty minutes into the meeting, he pulls out his phone and notices his TrickyDick account has seven responses. This looks very encouraging.

Once the meeting concludes, Rick races back to his legislative office to check out the responses. By the time he is back on his computer, the number of responses has grown to eleven. He starts to browse through them. He has a good laugh when he reads the first one.

I'm a married woman and my worm of a husband hasn't got the balls to give me the spice that I want...would you pull down my panties and spank me?

Well, this confirms that not everyone appreciates what strictly platonic means. Definitely not Muse material.

Hello to whom this may concern,
I am already smiling as I write this email. I see the potential in a confidante... I used to chat with a woman on the bus when I was a kid going to school about a variety of topics....I still think about her and where she is at. We had some great discussions.

Rick sighs. His first thought is that this woman doesn't really understand what he is looking for. He wants a Muse, not a friend. He is stunned when he reads the next email.

Hi there, nice to meet you. My name is Adele, age 31. Im an american and Ive been having serious issues in my own country. People have begun harassing me constantly, calling me a 'jew' and 'faggot.' Men and women have started assaulting me with their auras-agitating and molesting my body, head and genitals. It does not happen every once in awhile by one or another person, its been going on constantly, every waking moment and sometimes while I sleep, by almost every person who crosses my path. The remaining living members of my immediate family, all of them, have fallen in line. Do people behave this way in your country? Because if I am free from attack I would be happy to work for you.

They've got to keep this woman away from sharp objects, he tells himself as he hit the delete button.

Then an email catches his eye.

Would you be interested in chatting with a woman who very much wants this as well?

It is short and sweet but seems to resonate with him. He decides to reply.

So why do you very much want to be a Muse?

Three minutes later a response pops up in his inbox.

The muse resonates within me. Secretly I've always wanted to be the reason for another's inspiration...reason to smile...a confidante...in a purely non expectant relationship that is openly accepting.

This is precisely what he is looking for. This person seems to understand the role of a Muse. Someone who gives but expects nothing in return. Is she a crazy like the others? Rick decides he needs to continue the dialogue.

Well I think you are the first person who understands what I'm looking for.

Within a minute of responding, another email arrives in his inbox.

:) Would you like to speak to me?

Yes I think I would.

My number is 416-555-5125.

Rick thinks about it for a few minutes and decides this isn't a good time. He has promised to meet Lois for dinner. It will have to wait.

I will call you in the morning. Bye.

CHAPTER 27

**"We believe that to err is human.
To blame it on someone else is politics."
Hubert H. Humphrey**

When Rick arrives at the office in the morning, he checks his anonymous accounts and finds dozens of new responses to his ad. He decides he needs to delete the ad. He also finds an email from the Muse with the subject "Inspiration of the Day".

Good Morning! As your Muse, I have taken it upon myself to provide you with an inspirational message every morning. This is your first one.

Kitty

"Everyone wants to live on top of the mountain, but all the happiness and growth occurs while you're climbing it."

He smiles and looks up her number to call her. "Good morning, Kitty. Thanks for that inspirational message."

"Mmm. I was wondering if you were going to actually call me. I'm glad you did."

"By the way, I'm Rick."

"My real name is Katrina but I go by Kitty. I think the name better reflects my persona."

"How so?"

"Mmm. I'm very playful. So are kittens. What do you do, Rick? Are you an artist? Is that why you are looking for a Muse?"

"Well, I'm not sure I want to reveal too much about myself quite yet."

"Rick, I'm your Muse. Everything you say will always be held in complete confidence. I'm here for you."

"Hmm. Well, I'm a politician not an artist. But politicians need to be inspired as much as an artist."

"Oh, that is so cool! I find powerful men to be very sexy. What do politicians do?"

"It's a lot of boring stuff, really. And a lot of bullshit. Tell me about yourself."

"I'm a thirty-one year old free spirit. I don't believe in full-time work. I don't like to be tied down. I find part-time jobs and when I save enough money, I use it for travel. I want to see the world."

"Why the interest in being a Muse?"

"I like the idea of a secret relationship. It's so mysterious. Being part of someone else's life. I want to be able to excite someone's creative passion. I believe that a muse in her purest aspect is the feminine part of the male artist, with which he must have sexual intercourse if he is to bring into being a new work. I'm open to a physical relationship."

"Umm, that isn't part of my plan. The sex part, at least. I'm a married man."

"That's all right, Rick. I just want you to know I'm ready to inspire you in every way."

"I'm not sure yet how this is going to work but I'm sorry to disappoint you: there isn't going to be any sex. Maybe we could meet some time for coffee and a chat."

"I would love that. As your Muse, I will be available to you twenty-four hours a day. Just say the word."

"That's very considerate. First, let's see if there is any compatibility. How about we meet for coffee on Thursday afternoon. I will text you a location."

"Sweet. I will send you a photo so you can spot me. Looking forward to meeting you."

"Same here. Bye."

Several minutes later Rick receives a text message with a photo attached. The photo is of a woman from the waist up wrapped in a towel. She obviously took the photo right after getting out of the shower. She has wet dark brown hair that goes past her shoulders, large brown eyes and an olive complexion. There is a message is with the photo.

You've seen me now. There is more of me to see.
Looking forward to seeing you. :)

Rick sits there for a couple of minutes admiring the photo. Then he realizes that she may be getting the wrong impression. Her text and photo are very suggestive despite the fact that he has been clear about his intentions. He begins to feel some discomfort and deletes the photo from his phone.

Rick suddenly remembers he needs to be in the House and rushes over to the Legislative Building. Today is opposition day which is a day set aside by the Legislature for the opposition parties to set the agenda. On opposition days, the Liberals and NDP choose the subjects for debate. Auto insurance is expected to be one of the items for debate. As he takes his seat, the Premier gives Rick a wink that he takes as a sign that auto insurance is next on the agenda. At the moment, there is a Liberal member ranting about the expansion of slot machines in the province, by the government. The Minister of Consumer Relations responds to the Liberal member. The NDP member for Nickel Belt is next to be recognized by the Speaker. "Speaker, you know I have some strongly held views on the issue of auto insurance. It was remarkable that just earlier this week, we were talking about one-armed bandits when the Minister of Consumer Relations announced that this province was going to be infested in short order with slot machines. I mention this because it's not inappropriate to say that we should be discussing the two-armed banditry of the insurance industry in the same week as the Minister of Consumer Relations speaks of one-armed banditry.

"I know the Auto Insurance Reform Secretariat has received submissions from a number of people across the province, among others a document called Highway Robbery, which is why I don't hesitate to refer to the auto insurance industry as the two-armed bandits of Ontario in contrast to the one-armed bandits that the Minister of Consumer Relations wants to see in every corner of every block of every city, village and town in the province, so that every desperate, sad Ontarian can keep plunking their nickels, dimes, quarters and loonies into them in hopes of the big payoff, which of course will never happen.

"During the election campaign Rick Tompkins, the Minister responsible for Auto Insurance Reform blurts out, 'Oh, we have a plan to reduce auto insurance premiums.' Holy zonkers. That sent the spin doctors and the media relations people and the scriptwriters and the handlers and the keepers running and scrambling. Tompkins was scooped up. There were people nearby who thought there had been an abduction, the way Rick Tompkins was carried off by these Conservative hacks and thrown into the back seat of the limo, as it sped off. They were going: 'What the heck are you talking about? You've got a plan to reduce auto insurance premiums?' I'm sure Mr. Tompkins probably said, 'Well, don't we?' It was one of those: 'Huh? We must have one if I said it' moments.

"How does an insurance company make money? Simple proposition. When you're a profit-motivated insurance company, how do you make money, Speaker? I see you've got pen in hand, you're doing the calculation. You know darn well how you make money if you're a private, profit-motivated, corporate sector auto insurance company. You charge the maximum amount of premiums and pay out the least amount of benefits. It's an industry that, by its very nature, has to have short arms and deep pockets to make the maximum amount of profits. Not only do they have short arms and deep pockets, they also have short memories, because it was the auto insurance industry that fought for the system we have today.

"I heard the Minister say we are on the way to getting there. The problem is he didn't tell us where we are going because he doesn't know where we're going. Getting where? The idea is to provide fair, affordable auto insurance. Fair to drivers; affordable, which is implicit in fair; and fair to innocent accident victims. What you guys have done is crawl into bed with the private, for-profit automobile insurance industry — like I told you before, this is no queen-size bed, this is a king-size bed, because there's room for the Tories on one side and the Liberals on the other. It is a ménage à trois, an unholy trinity. The problem is that at the end of the day, who gets screwed? It's the drivers and the innocent accident victims. They're the ones getting the shaft."

When she sits down Rick rises to respond. "Speaker, the member from Nipissing has a wild imagination. She imagines kidnappings, conspiracies and sexual liaisons. I think she's been watching too much daytime TV. Somebody should check her attendance record. Or maybe someone needs to check what she is smoking." His comments initiate spontaneous jeering from the

Opposition side.

The Speaker interjects. "I will eject anyone who disrupts the business of this House."

Rick continues when the noise subsides. "The Conservative Party is the only party that has recognized that auto insurance is in crisis. Premiums are too high. We are the only party that has committed to doing something about it. We aren't going to lower rates by three percent or five percent. Who is going to notice that? We are committed to lowering premiums by twenty-five percent!" Rick pauses as the Government side breaks out into loud table banging. The Speaker again warns members that he will eject anyone disrupting the house. "This didn't come about by accident, as suggested by the Opposition member. It isn't some spin. It is the result of feedback from my own constituents, as well as voters from across the province. And we do have a plan. That plan will be announced at an appropriate time in the future."

When Rick sits down, he has a big grin. He looks over and notices that the Premier is giving him the thumbs up. At the end of the day's sitting, he makes his way out of the Chambers while a number of Conservative backbenchers are slapping him on the back. However, Rick is wondering what the plan is. So far, nothing is materializing from the Secretariat.

CHAPTER 28

**"If there's anything a public servant hates
to do it's something for the public." Kin Hubbard**

Rick is reviewing his agenda and day file, which is organized by Barbara. Ameena 3 has set up a meeting with a ratepayers group for mid morning and then he has house duty for the afternoon. He is relieved to have a very light agenda. He had promised to meet the Muse today.

Barbara appears at his door. "Minister, some of the group has already arrived and I've let them into the boardroom. Ameena 3 is here and wants to go over the meeting agenda with you."

"That's fine. Tell her to come in."

Moments later, Ameena 3 plops down in a chair in front of Rick's desk. "Good morning, Boss."

"Morning. Who are these people coming to annoy me today?"

"It's the East Brampton Ratepayers Association. They are looking for your support at Cabinet on a number of issues."

"Like what? More cricket pitches for Brampton?"

She frowns. "No Boss. This is a serious group of community activists."

"Stop calling me Boss."

"The association will be raising the need for more rapid transit, under funding on social services and a second hospital for Brampton."

"Am I in favor of these things?"

The frown returns to her face. "Yes, you are. Your day file has notes on all these issues."

"Okay, let me know when they are all here. In the meantime, I'll flip through the file."

After Ameena 3 leaves, Rick checks his phone for messages. He finds today's "Inspiration of the Day" from the Muse.

You can't start the next chapter of your life, if you keep rereading the last one.

Rick texts Kitty.

Thanks for the inspiration. I'm still available this morning. Let's meet at 11. The Starbucks on Bloor Street just east of Avenue Road, inside the Chapters.

Soon after, his phone chirps.

Sweet!

About fifteen minutes later, Barbara comes back to let Rick know he can head into boardroom. He picks up his files and walks into the adjoining room where the guests are all seated. "Good morning. I appreciate you people coming all the way from Brampton to meet with me. I have to make this commute every day." He walks around the table to shake hands and do introductions.

Once they are all seated again, the President of the Association begins his presentation. "Minister, thank you for finding time in your schedule to meet with us. The East Brampton Ratepayers Association is a volunteer organization that has been in existence for sixteen years. We have worked with politicians at the different levels of government to assist them in identifying priorities in our community. As a long-time resident of Brampton, I'm sure much of what you hear will not be new to you."

Rick looks down at his notes. "Yes. Yes, I may know a few things about these issues but go ahead."

"Brampton is the ninth largest city in Canada. It is larger than Quebec City, Regina, Halifax, Hamilton and London. Yet the provincial government still treats us like a sleepy bedroom community. We are lacking in infrastructure that exists in older cities. We have had numerous community meetings and have developed a short list of priority infrastructure projects for Brampton."

"As you have probably noticed, Brampton has some of the worst gridlock in Southern Ontario. Perhaps on the continent. We recognize that there is always going to be some level of gridlock, but if the problem gets much worse, then it will have a serious economic impact on the city. The busiest transportation corridor is between Mississauga and Brampton. We have been pushing for a light rail transit line for a number of years. No one suggests it isn't needed, however, the province has not yet committed to funding the project. Minister, we look to you to advocate for a regional LRT line with your Cabinet colleagues."

"So how much will this line cost?"

"Well over one billion dollars but it will depend on the length and how many stops."

"Ouch! That's a lot of money."

"It is but the region badly needs it. Minister, you are crusading for lower car insurance rates. You know that better transit options will take congestion off our roads and help lower rates."

"That's true. I will see what I can do to push for funding. What else do you want to talk about?"

"The next issue I want to bring to your attention relates to the population growth in Brampton. As you well know, we have just one hospital in the city, the Brampton Civic Hospital. Peel Memorial Hospital was shut down in 2007. The Civic is one of the busiest hospitals in Canada. Brampton residents are paying their share of taxes and the health premium but not getting the level of health services available elsewhere in Ontario. The provincial government has approved a second hospital but has not yet provided funding. Would you help us expedite the construction of the new hospital?"

"This sounds like another big ticket item."

"The cost would be about one-half billion."

"Well I'm on board on this one too. I will be pushing for funding approval."

"Thank you, Minister. Finally, another issue we've identified is the serious underfunding of social services in our city. Today, about 1.3 million people live in Peel. Of that number, it is estimated that thirty-three percent of new immigrants, twenty percent of children and forty percent of single seniors are living in poverty. Peel Region is still growing at a rate of 22,000 residents per year. The funding formulas aren't keeping up with that growth. With Mississauga pretty much built up, a good deal of the population explosion in Peel Region is occurring in Brampton. About a decade ago, Brampton's east end experienced a massive spike in population. Some neighborhoods in East Brampton have increased by almost 300 percent in just a five-year period. The region is getting shortchanged more than $300 million per year in per capita social services funding, compared to provincial averages. Minister, we need people like you to correct this inequity."

"Well I don't the like the idea of so many poor people in Brampton."

"Then you will support fairer funding?"

"Doesn't it make more sense to let the poor move to municipalities that provide more welfare and social services?"

"You can't be seriously suggesting that we export our poor?"

"Why not? It solves the underfunding problem and frees up dollars for these other projects."

"Minister, what you are suggesting is unthinkable. You would be turning your back on the most vulnerable members of the community."

"I'm thinking we could provide bus fare to wherever they would like to go. How's that for a helping hand?"

Ameena 3 realizes it's time to jump in. "Minister, I suggest that the Association send us some more information on this funding problem so we can better understand it."

Rick looks down at his phone and notices it's after 11:00 am. "Yes. Send us some stuff to look at. We need to wrap up anyways. I have an outside appointment that I'm late for.

There are several text messages from Kitty. He quickly texts her back.

Running a little late. On my way.

———

When Rick arrives at Starbucks, it is well after 11:00 a.m. All the tables are filled and the coffee drinkers have spilled over into the Chapters store. He looks around and finds whom he is searching for. Rick approaches a dark-haired woman who is busy with her phone. She is petite and exotic looking with large, luminous, hazel eyes. She has a natural olive and golden hue to her skin and long, dark, chocolate brown hair. "So I finally get to meet my Muse."

She looks up and smiles, "Hello Minister Tompkins. I'm so glad you showed up."

"Please call me Rick."

"And you can call me Kitty," she replies with a sly grin.

She notes some hesitation and adds, "You look nervous."

"A little."

"I won't bite, unless you ask me to."

Kitty leans forward and whispers, "I'm really excited to finally meet you."

"I've also been looking forward to this meeting. And you have such a sultry voice."

"I'm pleased that you find me attractive."

"I want to stress that this is a platonic relationship. I'm just looking for advice and some inspiration." Rick feels some discomfort, which causes him to shift around in his chair and drop his gaze.

"Yes I know, but as I told you over the phone I am open to all types of adventures that might stimulate your creativeness."

"Umm... that won't be necessary."

Kitty coos. "You don't want to hurt my feelings, do you?"

"Of course not." One of her legs is now strategically situated between his legs. His eyes dart around to see if anyone is listening in on the conversation. "Look, maybe you've misinterpreted my ad."

"You're looking for a Muse for inspiration. I'm prepared to inspire you using every tool I have at my disposal." She is now pouting.

"I think we need to discuss some ground rules."

"Sure, but remember, rules are made to be broken." Rick frowns. She lets out a sigh. "All right, I'll be good."

"I would love to know more about you. You told me you don't like working full-time. So what type of work are you doing right now?"

"Right now I'm not working. But I'm looking for some good opportunities."

"What types of jobs have you had in the past?"

"I never have problems finding work. Sometimes it finds me. I worked once as the personal assistant to the musical director of a symphony. I've worked in bars. The tips are amazing. I worked for an event planner. For a few months, I was a cheerleader for the Toronto Argos. I love to dance. Let's see, I've spent some time sorting mail at the Post Office."

"That's quite the resume you got there. What do you think you will do next?"

A big grin breaks out. "Gee, maybe I'll run for office. Maybe I'll run against you in the next election."

"Ha ha. I think you might manage to collect some votes."

"I might need to learn a few things about politics first. If I hang around you, I might pick up a few things. TrickyDicky, do you need an assistant?"

"Well if you are serious about helping me then maybe it makes sense to have you on staff."

"Are you serious? That would be so cool!"

"Let me check this out at the office. I'm not sure if I can hire another person but, if not, maybe you could be an unpaid intern until a position opens up. How does that sound?"

"Kitty likes the sound of it. Kitty would love to be working with TrickyDicky."

Rick gets up to leave. "I'll get back to you when I know

something."

Kitty follows him out and as they reach the street she gives Rick a hug and softly kisses him on the cheek. "Thanks for the coffee."

Rick makes his way through the throngs of tony shoppers carrying bags from Holts and Prada on Bloor Street's 'Mink Mile', where the average retail space rents for $300 per square foot. He turns down Bay Street and heads south back to his office. As he walks toward the entrance of his building, he spots Jerry coming out. "Hey Jerry! Do you have a minute?"

Jerry looks up from his BlackBerry. "I'm running late for a meeting. What's up?"

"I'm thinking of bringing someone into the office to work on some special projects. What's the process for hiring?"

"We have no budget dollars for another person. What special projects do you have?"

"Look you have your meeting. We can talk when you get back."

"Okay." Jerry continues to walk to the Whitney Block for a meeting at the Premier's Office. He has been invited to a confidential meeting on the Auto Insurance Review. He is relieved that Rick did not ask where he is going. Jerry has been instructed to keep the existence of the meeting from Rick since it is intended to discuss how to keep the review alive, as well as to decide on the fate of the Minister. When he arrives at the sixth floor offices of the Premier, he is directed to a small meeting room where the usual cast of purveyors of political advice has already assembled.

Geneva looks up from the power seat at the head of the table. "Have a seat, Switzer. We are just about to start." Jerry slides into the available seat at the table as Geneva begins the discussion. "Jerry, sorry to put you on the spot here but we are hearing that there are problems at the Secretariat. Maybe you can provide us with an update on the review."

Jerry sighs and looks around the table. The room has the feel of a shark's tank at dinnertime. "The Secretariat has completed its consultations on possible reforms. Essentially they have come up with blanks. The twenty-five percent commitment can't be done without a complete overhaul of the system, which would likely include a takeover of the insurance market by the government."

Leslie Geko has a question. Jerry remembers her from the campaign. She is now director of policy in the Premier's Office. She likely has his old job. "Can't we cut benefits to get our twenty-five percent?"

"It's impossible to achieve. No-fault benefits make up about one-third of the cost of auto insurance. You would essentially have to cut most of the benefits to save twenty-five percent."

Geneva is glaring at Jerry. "So this government made a commitment that it cannot possibly deliver?"

"Pretty much."

"We allowed some moron to hijack the party's agenda during an election. He makes a bullshit promise that we endorse. We then make him a Cabinet minister where he makes a complete ass of himself."

"I would say that is a pretty good summary of how we got here."

Her face is now as red as her curly mane. Her volume rises rapidly. "Switzer, you were supposed to be on top of this guy. How the fuck did you let this happen?"

"Me? I didn't propose making auto insurance reforms a central piece of the party's platform! I never suggested putting this guy into Cabinet. If we had listened to industry experts, we could have avoided this mess. You can't pin this on me."

Leslie jumps in. "Let's avoid finger pointing. We need to

figure out how to get out of this situation. Does anyone have any ideas?"

Karim Reza, who is in charge of issue management in the Premier's Office, speaks up. "Isn't the best political solution to make Tompkins the fall guy? We fire him and pin this all on him. The government appoints a new minister who comes back with a plan to reduce premiums but at a realistic level. I admit we take some lumps here but the next election is still far away and by then lower insurance rates will have trickled down to voters."

Leslie is shaking her head. "I don't see how we can walk away without getting hammered in this scenario. Rick Tompkins didn't make auto insurance rate reductions an election issue. We did. We can fire him for incompetence but we still wear it."

Geneva has cooled off from her blow up. "Let's try to buy ourselves some time. We are in the budget cycle now and don't want this shit taking attention away from our economic plan." She looks towards Lina Nesterov, the Premier's communications director. "Lina, is there some type of auto announcement we can make to make it look like we are making progress on this file?"

"I don't think we have anything to throw out there right now."

Jerry steps in. "Look, this isn't much but it's something. There is an online consumer guide that we have available on how to shop for auto insurance. We did an announcement a few months ago when a drunk Rick in Regina ended up on YouTube. We could do a bit of a rewrite and make it into a brochure on how to save money when shopping for auto insurance. Give it a slick cover and make some announcement. Chances are nobody will remember that we used it already."

Lina responds. "It might work. We can have a Conservative backbencher ask the Minister a question on auto insurance. I think that's how we worked it last time. He responds by announcing the consumer guide which will assist consumers with saving on their insurance, while the government is working on reforms."

Geneva looks around the room. "Has anyone got a better idea?" No one responds. "Then I guess we go with this. Lina, let's get this brochure pulled together by the end of the week. And Switzer? Good one."

CHAPTER 29

"The chief cause of problems is solutions."
Eric Sevareid

It is particularly early for Rick to be at his desk. It's before 8:00 a.m. and only Jerry is in the office. Rick is having a coffee and reading the news clippings distributed by the Secretariat's communications staff. He notices that a columnist in the *Toronto Star* has a piece where he is speculating on how the government's auto insurance review is coming along. The columnist comments how much public interest there is on the plans to bring down high auto insurance premiums. The past few days have begun to gnaw away at Rick. He did not expect this project to be so damn difficult. No one is really cooperating with him on this. Rick checks his phone for messages. He finds another "Inspiration of the Day" from the Muse.

Am I lying to you if I tell you the same lie I tell myself?

It's been a couple of days since he met with Kitty and he decides it might be a good time to raise the possibility of a position for her, with Jerry. He pokes his head into Jerry's office. "Have you got a couple of minutes?"

"Sure, come on in. I was actually just about to pop over to

go over something with you."

"What's that?"

"The Premier's Office is unhappy with the progress on the review and would like something to announce."

"But we've got nothing."

"Well, the Premier's Office is developing a consumer brochure on how to save money shopping for auto insurance. They are also developing a marketing plan for the brochure. The plan is to have a friendly question directed to you in the House from one of our backbenchers, which you will use as an opportunity to announce the brochure. The thinking is this might possibly give us some goodwill while we work out how to get out of this mess."

"Haven't we done this already?"

"Yes and we're hoping no one will notice."

"Will it work?"

"Who knows? The announcement will happen in a few days. I'll give you some speaking notes." Jerry returns to the original conversation. "So what is it you wanted to talk about?"

"I would like to do some independent research on some of the options raised by the Secretariat. Not that I don't trust them but it's good to gather as much information as possible to make the right decision. You mentioned that we have no money to hire someone. But what about an unpaid intern? It could be a developmental opportunity for this person."

"Sounds like you have someone in mind for this," says Jerry, giving Rick his full attention and sounding just a little suspicious.

"There is an acquaintance whom I would like to help by providing some work experience."

"How long would this so-called internship last?"

"Let's say three or four months. Would that be a problem?"

"This is your office. You don't need my permission. Just a

word of advice. You don't need any more things blowing up on you. You might not survive the next one."

"Understood. But there aren't going to be any problems."

When Rick gets back to his office, he texts Kitty.

I didn't forget about you. I can't get you a paid position but if you are interested in an unpaid internship you might learn a lot here. Let me know what you think.

She quickly texts back.

OMG I would luv to do this! Thx!
Would you like to come over for dinner to discuss?

Rick agrees.

I should be able to make it. Would 7 pm work? Send me your address.

Moments later she responds.

7 is cool :)
3707 highborne ave #1604 door code is 323

He sends her a final text.

See you then.

Before putting away his phone, Rick sends a text to Lois.

Got a meeting this evening.
Will be home as soon as I can.

Rick heads down to the underground parking to get his car. He keys Kitty's address into his car's GPS and discovers the address is in suburban North York. When he arrives at Kitty's apartment complex, he walks to the entrance of the tired looking building. This is not what he expected from a Muse. He approaches the intercom and punches in 323, which unlocks the exterior door. When he reaches the lobby elevators, he hits the UP button. While waiting for an elevator to reach the ground floor, he notices a couple of signs posted in the lobby. One sign announces that a fire evacuation drill would take place at 11:00 a.m. on Thursday. The other sign provides a list of floors that will be getting the hallway carpets replaced and on what dates.

When the elevator finally arrives, Rick quickly steps inside and pushes the button for the sixteenth floor. He steps out when the elevator stops and quickly concludes that this is not one of the floors that has undergone carpet replacement. The brown carpets are visibly worn and greying. There is an occasional stain and the carpeting has a slight musty smell, similar to what you would expect from a wine cellar.

When Rick reaches unit 1604, he knocks lightly on the door, trying to be as inconspicuous as possible. As he waits for the door to open, an elderly woman pops out of the unit two doors over and shuffles down the hall. He can feel her eyeballing him as he nervously stares down at the stained carpet. Finally, the door swings open and he steps inside.

Kitty leans forward and kisses his cheek. He scans the apartment which has little in the way of furniture. The living room has a rust colored three-seat sofa with a matching chair. In front of the sofa is a tan ottoman and on top of that is a large green tray holding an assortment of nail polishes, nail lacquers, files and tools that he is unable to identify. Rick gazes down and notices her toenails have a fresh coat of blue polish. He assumes that she has just given herself a pedicure. His eyes return to scanning the apartment. The living room also has a forty-six inch TV but no other furniture, which makes the parquet floor look almost naked. There are beige vertical blinds on the windows that are almost the same colour as the dull apartment walls. The dining room has no furniture other than a wall-to-wall bookcase that is crammed with books.

It is at that moment that he notices what Kitty is wearing - a tight black skirt that highlights her generous curves and a sheer black blouse with no bra that is only partially buttoned up. She notices him staring. "I hope you don't mind how I dressed. I just felt sexy this evening."

"Umm, it's fine. But you can't dress like this in the office."

She smiles. "Of course not. I just thought you might enjoy seeing this side of me. I can be very professional. Would you like a drink? I have some wine for dinner but you can have something else if you'd like."

"Wine would be fine." He follows her into the kitchen. There is no visible counter space. It seems every dish, pot, kitchen utensil, can and bottle in the kitchen is out on the counters. There is a tiny eating area with a small round glass table and two chairs. On the table is an open bottle of Sterling Pinot Noir from California and two wine glasses. Rick picks up the bottle. "I like your taste in wine."

"Why don't you pour us both a glass while I finish dinner. I hope you're hungry."

He pours wine into the two glasses and walks over to hand one to her. "Cheers." He takes a sip from his glass. "I'm starved actually."

"By the way, I'm a vegan. I made an organic spinach salad with a homemade dressing and a lentil and brown rice casserole. I hope you are alright with that."

"It sounds delicious." He forces a smile although the dish sounds absolutely awful. What's with these dumb-ass vegans?

"Have a seat and I'll serve the salad." Kitty brings two plates of salad to the table. Ricks looks down at the salad. The spinach looks slimy and the edges of the leaves are brown.

"The salad is great." He has to make himself smile again, while forcing a forkful of the slimy mess into his mouth. The dressing is so sour he has to struggle to keep from puckering up. He tries to wash it all down with wine and has a sense of relief when he finally clears his plate.

"Rick, would you like some more?"

"Umm, no I want to save room for the main course." He knows he should have stopped and grabbed a bite to eat before coming over.

"Great. I think it's ready to be served." She gets up to pull the casserole out of the oven. As she bends over Rick can make out her hanging breasts through her scanty top and finds himself staring again. She spoons out two servings onto plates and brings them to the table.

Rick looks down at this plate, trying to figure out what he is about to put in his mouth. The casserole looks like gruel. "This looks great!" He gingerly brings his fork to his mouth and deposits it inside. The casserole is undercooked and the lentils have the consistency of gravel. Even worse, it tastes like wallpaper paste. Rick struggles to keep from gagging, as he reaches for his wine glass.

"Rick, I see you're really enjoying the wine. I can barely keep up. Would you like me to open another bottle?"

"No, no, this is fine. You know, I'm actually not that hungry after all."

"You didn't like it?"

"I'm more of a burger and fries type of guy."

"I can make you something else."

"It's fine. I really came over to talk about the position in my office. I can tell you what it is and you can decide if you are interested."

"I would love to hear about it. Why don't we sit in the living room, where it's more comfortable." She gets up from the kitchen table and leads Rick to the living room. Rick finds a spot on the sofa. Kitty sits down facing him with their knees just touching. "So tell me about this internship."

"Here is my plan. I can bring you in as an unpaid intern for three months, maybe four. You can do some independent research for me. It will involve internet searches and interviewing people. You summarize what you've found out and maybe down the road, a permanent job will open up. Does this sound like something you would be interested in?"

"Sounds like fun. I think I can manage it for a few of months. Though you know a permanent gig is just not my style. I don't like to be tied down. I want to be able to take off whenever I want. Try new things. You know I'm a free spirit. I gotta be able to spread my wings."

"Okay. Fair enough."

She nuzzles a little closer. "I'd love to spread my wings around you right now." She leans forward, which provides Rick with an almost unobstructed view of her generous cleavage. While he is distracted by the scenic view, she moves on top of Rick and locks her lips onto his.

Ricks jumps up off the sofa. "Now that I'm your boss, we can't have any of this. I'm sorry but I have to get going."

"Oh, what a shame. We were just starting to have some fun."

She is now pouting.

Rick quickly heads out the door towards the elevator. When he gets to the ground floor, he makes a beeline for his car and heads home.

CHAPTER 30

"Nothing is so admirable in politics as a short memory." John Kenneth Galbraith

In the morning, Kitty gets up early for her first day of work at the Minister's office. She is conservatively dressed in black slacks and an emerald green sweater. She exits the Wellesley subway station and the bright sunlight makes her squint. She pulls out her sunglasses from her purse and puts them on. As she focuses on her surroundings, she begins to walk down Wellesley towards Bay Street. The sidewalk is busy with people scurrying to work. No doubt they are running late. As she nears Bay Street, she makes out a bearded man sitting cross-legged on the sidewalk. Beside him are two dogs - one appears to be asleep, the other is drinking water from a bowl. The man is holding a sign in his lap: 'Options Limited Due To Poor Decisions.' She stops and looks down at the man who is wearing a dirty grey t-shirt and khaki pants. "I love dogs. What are their names?"

"The white dog is Paco and the brown one is Tramp."

"They look very gentle." She pulls out a five dollar bill from her wallet and places it in the man's pail that is in front of him.

"Thank you, ma'am!"

Kitty turns around and returns to Yonge Street and locates a small grocery store. A few minutes later, she returns to the panhandler with a bag of dog treats. "Can I give them some treats?"

He looks a little surprised. "Sure."

She tears open the bag and hands each dog some treats. She then hands over the bag to the man. "Have a good day."

"You too, ma'am. You're very kind."

When Kitty gets off the Ferguson Block elevator on the fourth floor, she turns towards the Minister's office. When she reaches Barbara's desk, she asks for Minister Tompkins. Moments later Rick comes out to greet her and brings her into his office. "You look so important behind that big desk. It's very sexy."

"Look, you can't be talking like that in the office. You are going to have to be discreet for this to work."

"Yes, of course. But the door is closed. We could be humping on your desk and no one would be the wiser." She bats her big brown eyes in Rick's direction.

"We are going to keep things strictly business in the office. There will be no one on the desk. You aren't going to be talking about any humping on my desk. Is that clear?"

She straightens up in her chair and salutes. "Yes Minister!"

"We need to come up with a story on how we know each other."

"How about we were introduced by a mutual friend."

"Good idea. I'm going to walk you over to meet Jerry. He's my executive assistant and will go over the research assignment that you'll be taking on." They get up and walk across the hall to Jerry's office. "Good morning Jerry. This is Katrina, our new intern I told you about."

Jerry gets to his feet and shakes her hand. "Nice to meet you Katrina and welcome to Queen's Park. Why don't you have a seat and make yourself comfortable?"

"Thank you. I prefer to be called Kitty." She looks around at Jerry's office, which is much smaller and considerably less tidy that Rick's. She finds a seat without a stack of papers on it.

Rick heads out the door. "I'm headed to the Legislative Building. Jerry will show you around and set you up."

Jerry leans back in his chair trying to size up the new intern. "Have you had any experience in a political office before?"

"No. I find this very exciting."

"Yeah, it can be exciting. So how do you and the Minister know each other? Is there some type of insurance connection?"

She hesitates, trying to think of something that won't raise any suspicion. "Well, I've always been interested in politicians and politics and I needed a job. I was introduced to the Minister through a friend and just asked whether there were any opportunities available. And here I am."

"Okay. I'm going to walk you around the office and introduce you to the others and show you to your desk. We are cramped for space so you won't have an office but then you are only here a short time. I'll bring you some research that needs to be done once you get settled."

As they are about to get up, Lawrence pops his head in the office. "Do you have a minute, Jerry? I have a couple of questions about the brochure release today."

"Hi Lawrence. I want to introduce you to our new intern, Kitty."

Lawrence shakes Kitty's hand. "It's great to get another body in here. Hmm...is your perfume Chanel Allure?"

"Yes it is. It's one of my favorite scents."

"I love it too. I recognized it because I usually wear Allure Homme. I also use the body wash."

"Me too. I also bathe with milk. In fact, I recently switched to goat's milk."

"That's awesome."

Jerry jumps in. "May I remind you two that government

offices are supposed to be fragrance free. Kitty, let me finish showing you around and the two of you can exchange aesthetics tips later on."

———

Down the street in the Legislative Building, Question Period is well underway. There are no significant bills to be introduced and attendance in the House is sparse. Eventually, a question is directed to Minister Tompkins from Daniel McClintock, a Conservative backbencher. "My question is for the Minister responsible for Auto Insurance Reform. My constituents are looking forward to lower auto insurance rates in the near future. Could the Minister update the members on what the government is doing to bring down the cost of auto insurance for drivers in Ontario?"

Rick has a prepared answer for the planted question. "Thank you for your question. Your question happens to be very timely. The government is about to launch a new consumer guide on how to save money when purchasing auto insurance. This new guide will be available online and in hard copy and will provide very helpful tips for consumers on how to pay less for their insurance. The government intends on having the paper version of the brochure available at government offices, including all drivers testing centers and ServiceOntario centers. All drivers will benefit further, later in the year, when the government introduces reforms to save them even more money."

McClintock rises to respond. "Thank you Minister, for that update. My constituents will be pleased to find out that the government is moving ahead to make auto insurance more affordable. I'm sure all drivers will be looking forward to lower auto insurance premiums."

The opposition members on the other side of the House witness this exchange with either bored looks or smirks. However, no one bothers to stand up to question the Minister any further regarding his reform initiative. Jerry watches it from his office on the Ontario Parliamentary cable channel. He's pleased to see that the opposition has totally ignored it. There will be a press release on the brochure going out shortly that will probably generate some news items. There are always enough lazy reporters that will use it to file a story, even if they know it's just government spin.

When Rick returns to his office, Ameena 3 is waiting for him. He ushers her into his office. "So what's the word from the wonderful citizens of Bramalea-Gore-Malton?"

"I have a few things for you, Boss. I mean, Minister. First, there are a number of congratulatory letters for you to sign that will be sent to constituents. I have four milestone anniversary letters and nine birthday letters."

"Do I really have to sign these things? Can't you just use a signature stamp?"

"No, I can't. The letters are supposed to be personalized. How personal is a stamp?"

"What else do you have for me? Let me guess. Someone wants to know if they can raise chickens in their backyard?"

"No. Nothing like that. I need to schedule you to make appearances for some upcoming Sikh festivals and an Islamic holiday. Lawrence and I will work out some short speaking notes for you."

"Oh brother. Why can't these people just celebrate Christmas and Easter and make things simpler?"

"Oh my god! I hope you aren't being serious."

"Yeah, look who I'm talking to: Ameena 41, or whatever number you are going by this week."

"It's always been Ameena 3. We also need to schedule another town hall. I'm thinking the last week of the month. Before people disappear for the summer. Turn out is quite low when the weather turns nice."

"Sure. But where do you find such stupid people for these things? I swear everyone who comes out must work at the airport."

Ameena 3 sighs. "Not every Indian drives a cab or works at the airport. Believe it or not, some Indians have law and medical degrees."

"I'll take your word for it."

CHAPTER 31

"If you saw a heat wave, would you wave back?"
Steven Wright

Jacob looks up from his breakfast. "How is it today?"

Ameena 3 has an enormous smile. "Mmmm. This is still my absolute favorite breakfast of all time. I don't care about the lineups at this place. I love the Bloor West Village, especially in summer." She takes another bite from her baked french toast, stuffed with mascarpone cheese and strawberries. "I love that they use brioche instead of bread."

"You don't want to know how many calories are in that breakfast."

"Shut up, Jake! I'm having an oral orgasm. Don't ruin the moment."

"I bet you can't find breakfasts like this in Brampton."

"Nope. Breakfast at the office is a Tim Horton coffee and bagel."

"A Canadian classic," Jacob points out with a laugh.

"Did I tell you about our last town hall with the Minister?"

"No, you never mentioned anything about it."

"Probably because I get so frustrated and exhausted trying to manage the Minister. He is impossible."

"More politically incorrect comments?"

"Well for one thing, every guy who asked a question, he called Kumar."

"Why Kumar?"

"Probably from the Harold and Kumar movies. I'm guessing they're his type of movies."

"That must go over well."

"Well, that's really just par for the course. He always happens to have a stack of business cards for his insurance brokerage that somehow fall out of his pocket at some point in the evening. He lets out an 'oops' and then when picking them up, asks if anyone would like one."

"That is pretty tacky."

"More than just tacky. A Minister can't be promoting his business. That's a major conflict of interest. Did I tell you about the new woman in the Minister's office?"

"I don't think so."

"Her name is Kitty. She started last month, as an intern. A total ditz. I hear for the first couple of weeks, every time someone mentioned Cabinet she thought they were referring to the filing cabinets."

"How did she get hired?"

"She says they were introduced by a mutual friend of the Minister, whatever that means. Just something doesn't feel right about her. I mean she is really sweet but what is she doing in the Minister's office?"

"Maybe he was doing someone a favor by getting her the job?"

"Maybe. It's really strange. He brought her along to the town hall, though I have no idea why. Throughout the evening, she was fawning all over him. It was so awkward."

"Could they be having an affair?"

"Who knows? I asked Lawrence about her. He tells me that

he hasn't noticed anything. They are strictly professional in the office."

"Maybe you're just imagining it."

"I don't think so. This woman does not belong in the Minister's office."

———

Jerry is trying to pick up his pace but the crowds on the sidewalk keep slowing him down. It's Tuesday night but the bars and restaurants in Little Italy are still packed. Even in the evening, the heat and humidity make the air so heavy. His clothes cling to his clammy skin. But then, he perspires more than most people.

Evening traffic on College Street is always gridlocked with cars circling the neighborhood looking for a parking spot. The heat coming off of all those cars idling only contribute to the mugginess. When he finally arrives at La Gondola Restaurant, there is a lineup that snakes out the front door. He pushes his way through to the dining room and looks around. He spots Geneva at a table by a window.

"Switzer, I thought I was being stood up."

"Sorry, I lost track of time and then my phone died so I couldn't text you."

"I got a table inside because it's too humid and buggy to be sitting outside on the patio."

"Works for me. I hate the humidity."

"So what are you doing in the city during your vacation time. Don't you ever go away?"

"I only took the time off because the Minister is up north at his cottage for a few weeks, so the office is really quiet. Might as well take advantage of the downtime. I sometimes head up to the family cottage in Muskoka, but it's anything but quiet and relaxing. Right now, the entire family is up there and it's a zoo. This time of year, it's not so bad to be hanging out in the city. It tends to be pretty quiet although you wouldn't know from the crowds in Little Italy."

"Yeah, it's crazy out there."

A server stops at the table and looks at Geneva. "I see your guest has finally arrived." Jerry guesses that she has been complaining to the server about him being late. "Can I get you started with drinks?"

Jerry looks across at Geneva. "Are you alright with ordering a bottle of wine?" She nods in agreement. He looks up at the server. "We'll have a bottle of the Montepulciano."

"Switzer, what are you going to have?"

"I'm going with the spaghetti and meatballs."

"Ugh, how boring."

"I happen to like spaghetti and meatballs. What are you having?"

"I'm going to have the seafood risotto."

"How is rice any more exotic than spaghetti and meatballs?"

The server returns with their wine and pours them both a glass. Geneva takes a sip of her wine. "It just is, Switzer. Just like lemon ginger scones are more interesting than bagels and crème brûlée is more interesting than Jell-o."

"So, I have simple tastes."

"Switzer, I just love to push your buttons," she says and then laughs. "Let's get the business out of the way before we've had too much wine. Give me the latest on our auto insurance file. What has Minister Ned Flanders been up to?"

Jerry has a puzzled look. "Who?"

"Seriously? You've never seen The Simpsons?"

"Not recently."

She pulls out her phone and Googles 'Ned Flanders' and

holds up her phone so Jerry can see the picture she has found.

"Wow! That actually does look like Rick. As for work, maybe you need to have a few glasses in you before we talk about the file."

"Christ! Didn't I know this would get fucked up?"

"Nothing is fucked up. Not yet. But I just don't see how we can deliver on the rate reduction commitment. You just can't make twenty-five percent of the cost of insurance go away without doing some major surgery. But people are going to scream bloody murder if we begin to slash away at the product."

"You did months of consultations. Didn't anything come out of those meetings?'

He takes a big long sip of wine. "The process was informative but has produced very little that can be used to bring down rates."

"Why am I not surprised? We can't have this review go on forever. Maybe it's still early but at some point we need to begin planning an endgame: for the review and the Minister."

"I suppose."

"I'm not blaming you. The campaign team got blinded by polling numbers and shifted the game plan without thinking it through. At some point, we are going to have to take a hit over this."

"So what will happen to Rick? More important, what happens to me?"

"Rick will find himself in the backbenches with the other numbnuts who call themselves MPPs. Which is where he belongs."

"Sadly, Rick is just not Cabinet material. In fact, he's a crappy MPP. He has no interest in constituency work. His riding will be hard to hang on to."

"I agree. As for you? Well, I think I've gotten over our tryst from the fall. I could really use your talents in the Premier's office."

"Really? That sounds good to me."

"But only on one condition."

"What's that?"

"After dinner, we go our separate ways," she says with a grin.

"Ha! I'm with you on that."

"Enough shop talk. Let's not ruin the evening for you. Shit, you probably never even get fresh air." She smiles and raises her glass.

"Cheers"

"And I see the server coming this way with your spaghetti and meatballs."

━━━━━━━

The intense heat and the gentle rocking of the dock is making Rick very sleepy. The drone of motorboats on the lake fades in and out depending on their distance from Tompkins' cottage. He has spent almost ten minutes trying to get through page 102 of Stephen King's 11/22/63. His semi-sedated state is interrupted by the shock of cold water being dumped on his chest. He sits up and opens his eyes. "Hey!" He spots his son Kyle scampering up the path from the deck to the cottage.

Moments later, Lois shows up with a beer in her hand. "I thought you might want one of these."

"Thanks. I am getting thirsty."

"I saw Kyle tearing up the path. What was that about?"

"The brat decided to pour water on me. I guess I must have looked too comfortable and relaxed."

Lois sits down on the lounge chair next to Rick and pulls her bathing suit cover-up off over her head. "Hun, will you rub some sunscreen onto my back?"

"Sure." He grabs the bottle from her outstretched hand and sprays a thin layer of oily lotion onto her back. He rubs the sunscreen into her skin until the lotion disappears.

Lois lowers the lounge chair so that she can lie down on it on her stomach. She puts her head on a folded up beach towel and closes her eyes. "Are you still enjoying that book?"

"Oh yeah."

"I'm not into King's horror books."

"This one doesn't fall into his usually genre. It's about a time traveler who tries to prevent the Kennedy assassination. It's a very cool story." His phone chirps to notify him that he has a text. It's from Kitty.

Good Morning Minister!
Here is your inspirational message for the morning.
Your flesh is not a reflection of your soul. So when you look in the mirror, remember that your light outshines your flaws.

"Who is that?" asks Lois.

"Just someone in the office. You can never completely get away from the office with one of these things."

"Why don't people just turn them off when they don't want to be disturbed instead of bitching about it?"

"It's hard to explain," he says with a sigh.

Thanks. How are things in the office?

So quiet without you.
I'm sitting here imagining you in a tight pair of swimming trunks. :)

You are not.

Really I am. But of course I would be swimming nude.

Hmm. I bet you would.

Lois turns towards him looking a little annoyed. "Is that the same person texting you?"

"Umm...yes."

"Why don't you tell him to politely shove it?"

My wife says you should shove it lol

Mmm, I was thinking the same thing...

Now stop that you're supposed to be working

Yes boss lol.

"I've gotten rid of him."

"Good. Hun, are you looking to get into your wife's good book?"

"Oh? What do I have to do?"

"I need a bottle of water but I'm too comfy to get up. Be a good boy and get it for me?"

He gets up and walk off the dock towards the cottage. "Just like the office. Never any peace."

CHAPTER 32

"It is better to keep your mouth closed and let people think you are a fool than to open it and remove all doubt." Mark Twain

It is another dreary post-Labour Day Monday morning and Jerry is sitting at his desk thinking about how bleak things have gotten. The Minister is repeatedly stepping into muck and making a mess of things. In fact, if there were a clear path through the muck, he would probably still somehow step in it. This auto insurance file is sinking fast and might eventually sink the government as well. Jerry knows that he will somehow also wear it. What he needs now is a 'Hail Mary pass'. The problem is he is Jewish and doesn't know the Hail Mary prayer. Then his phone rings. "Good morning. Jerry Switzer here."

"Good morning, it's Margaret. How are you doing?"

"I'm okay but you could make things better with some good news."

"You must have been reading my mind."

"Don't tease a desperate man. I've been contemplating climbing out onto the ledge outside my window."

"Well, you may not need to jump."

"So what have you got for me?"

"I'm in my car. I'll be in the office in about an hour and can stop by if you are free to talk about it."

"I'm around all morning."

"Then I'll see you in a bit."

Jerry is doing a Google search for the Hail Mary prayer when Margaret shows up. He looks up from his screen. "Come in. I'm just looking up the Hail Mary prayer. I thought it might be an appropriate time to use it."

She looks puzzled. "I thought you were Jewish."

"Never mind. It's really a sports reference. Sit down and tell me what this is about."

"The Secretariat staff have continued to do some brainstorming and we have an idea to throw out there. I think, at this point, we have to consider anything and everything. I've brought you a briefing note outlining the idea. Read this and tell me what you think."

Jerry spends the next few minutes going over the note. When he is done, he leans back in his chair and lets it sink in before speaking. "This has some merit. Certainly worth exploring."

"I think so too."

"Do you have more details on this plan?"

"No, this is it. I wanted to run this by you first before spending more time fleshing it out. But if you're in agreement, then I can have my people begin to work on it immediately."

"Yes, go ahead. I'm not mentioning this to anyone quite yet. People are a little anxious about this file right now and I don't think we need any added pressure. When we have more details, we can set up some meetings to review it with others. I would like something back in two weeks time. Is that feasible?"

"We can do it."

"Let's keep this quiet for now. I owe you Margaret."

"Just doing my job."

Jerry looks at the time and realizes he is late for a lunch

meeting. He scrambles to get notes together and rushes out. As he walks out the door, he turns to let Barbara know that he will be out for the next few hours. But she isn't at her desk. He looks over at Kitty. "Where's Barbara?"

"She went home sick."

"Who is handling all the incoming calls?"

"I am. She asked if she could forward her calls to me before leaving. I said sure."

"Okay. I'll be back in a few hours, in case someone is looking for me."

She nods back to him as she responds to a call coming in. "Hello, Minister Tompkins' office."

"Hi. I'm Christie Lefebre, a reporter for the *Toronto Sun*. I am looking to set up some time with the Minister to do an interview with him."

"Hmm. I'm not quite sure who I should refer you to."

"Aren't you his secretary?"

"No, I'm just covering the phones for the afternoon."

"What's your name? What's your job in the office?"

"I'm Kitty. I haven't been here very long. I do some research and I'm also a Muse."

"You're a Muse?"

"Yes. You know what a Muse is? She exists to be the source of someone's inspiration."

"Yes, I do happen to know what a Muse is. But I'm curious, who would that someone be?"

"Well, right now, it's Minister Tompkins."

"That's very interesting. Umm, I really don't know much about being a Muse. I would love to sit down with you some time to discuss it."

"Really? I would be happy to talk to you about it."

"I happen to be free after work either today or tomorrow, if either day works for you."

"I'm free tomorrow."

"That's great. Why don't we meet at the bar at the Four Seasons at 5:30. I'll be holding a copy of the *Toronto Sun*. This will be so much fun."

"Looking forward to it...but what about the appointment with the Minister."

"Oh yeah, I'll call back another time to arrange it."

"Okay, see you tomorrow."

———

Graham Wallace from the Committee for Fair Auto Insurance and Chip Bonham from the Insurance Association of Canada are seated in the reception area outside of Rick Tompkins' office. It is after 5:00 p.m. and most of the staff have left for the day. Graham is on his phone speaking to his assistant. Chip is also on his phone, flipping through emails. Jerry pops his head out of the boardroom. "Sorry to keep you waiting. The Minister is now available to meet with you."

Rick gets up from his seat at the boardroom table. "Gentlemen, good to see you." They exchange handshakes before sitting down. The optics around the table are somewhat awkward. Graham and Chip are on one side dressed in banker blue suits, dark blue ties and blue shirts with white collars. Rick and Jerry are on the other side of the table wearing polyester suits and white shirts with open collars. "So what is this proposal that you would like to discuss with me?"

Graham speaks first. "First off, thank you Minister for agreeing to see us. In particular, since we've been rather secretive about the topic."

Rick has his usual smirk on his face. "Well, I assume it has something to do with auto insurance."

Graham continues. "Yes, of course. My group and the IAC have been secretly meeting for the past three months to see if we could reach some consensus on auto insurance reforms. We thought that it might be advantageous to the government if we were all on the same page. Well, I'm pleased to inform you that after some very intense negotiations, the plaintiff bar and the insurance industry have reached an agreement. I want to point out to you, Minister, that this is the first time we have been able to agree on reforms to the system."

Rick looks a little stunned by this news. "This is a pleasant surprise."

Chip takes over for Graham. "We have dubbed the plan Ex Novo, which is Latin for 'from new'. One of the things the lawyers are eager to see is better access to the courts for not at-fault victims. At the same time, the insurance industry wants to see no-fault benefits scaled back. So each side gave a little and took a little."

Rick turns to Jerry and can tell from the look on his face that he is quite pleased. He responds with an eyebrow raised. "Well, any plan going forward is going to be called 'The Road Ahead'..."

Graham jumps in. "Of course Minister. You can call it anything you like."

Rick continues. "Frankly, I can't believe the two of you could agree on what day it is let alone on a set of reforms. But this is great news. Chip, have you had the plan costed by industry actuaries?"

Chip is staring at his notes. "Yes. Well, it's not going to come in at the twenty-five percent that you've been looking for. By now we all know that's not realistic. But we are optimistic that we can get between ten and twelve percent savings, if the government implements the plan as set out in the note I will leave with you."

"Come on guys! Are you serious? Do you expect the government to meekly agree to ten percent savings? There is no goddamn way!"

Chip's tone becomes more hostile. "Minister, don't forget whatever package of reforms you come up with will need the insurance industry's cooperation if you expect to implement it."

Rick's face quickly changes to red from its normal tanned shade. "Really? That sounds like blackmail to me."

Jerry is beginning to panic. "Wait...Wait. Minister, let's first spend time going over their proposal." He quickly scoops up their note before Rick considers handing it back. "There may be some very useful ideas here. Maybe we can indeed use this as a starting point."

"Sure. Have the Secretariat staff take a look at this. But I'm not going to be caving in. We promised twenty-five percent and that's what we are going to deliver."

Graham gets up from his seat. "Thank you so much for your time, Minister. After you've had a chance to discuss our proposal internally, why don't we set up another meeting to discuss it."

After the two guests leave the boardroom, Jerry turns to Rick. "We need to seriously consider their proposal. All this bravado sounds nice but there is no chance you can come up with twenty-five percent savings."

"Hey, these guys are full of shit. If we hang tough, we can squeeze a lot more out of them."

Jerry vainly attempts to balance his file folder and two coffees in his hands while trying to push the sixth floor button, in the Whitney Block elevator. The only other person in the elevator notices him struggling and comes to his aid. When he gets to Geneva's office, he is almost bowled over by her as she darts out the door. "Grab a seat, Switzer. I'll be right back."

Jerry sits down at a round table in the corner of her office. On the table is a small vase with an arrangement of artificial flowers. As he gazes around the office, it strikes him that there is no paper in sight. How does she manage that, in the position she's in? His office has paper piled everywhere - on his desk, on furniture, on the floor. Geneva reappears and drops down in one of the chairs next to Jerry. "So your text last night indicated you wanted to discuss something urgent. What's up?"

"Oh, I brought you a coffee. Skim milk, no sugar." He hands her one of the coffees.

"Thanks."

"I wanted to bring you up to date on the latest developments regarding the insurance file. Late yesterday, the Insurance Association and the Committee for Fair Auto Insurance presented the Minister with a proposal the two groups have been working on jointly. The package of reforms they are endorsing would bring down rates by about ten to twelve percent. My sense is that this might be the best we can do. And it will have both the insurance industry and the plaintiff bar behind it."

"I think I see where you are going on this. We can deliver on half of the promised premium reductions. We will take some knocks from opponents and the media. The public will probably still be happy to save some money."

"Exactly. As an option, we can always suggest further work will be done to identify additional savings for the future. Leave the door open for more reductions."

"Do you have something for me to look at?"

He pulls a note out from his file folder and puts it down in front of her. "This is what they left us with."

"Okay, let me look this over and get back to you. This sounds very encouraging."

"I should mention that the Minister is not exactly in love with this proposal. He is still wedded to the original twenty-five percent commitment."

"The Premier's office will reach out to the IAC and the Committee for Fair Auto Insurance and negotiate directly with them. We can't have Minister Dipshit screwing things up. You can be there to represent the Secretariat."

"Whatever you want. I'm happy to assist."

"I really appreciate you bringing this to me. I'll keep in touch. Now I've got to run to another meeting. Take care, Switzer." She leaps out of her chair and bounds out the door leaving him sitting alone. He gets up and walks down the corridor back to the elevator. He intentionally didn't bring up the Secretariat's proposal. There's no point in raising any expectations before knowing if what they have suggested is feasible. Better to keep that under wraps for now.

━━━━━━━

At the end of the workday, Kitty makes her way north on Bay Street towards the Four Seasons Hotel on Yorkville. It's about a twenty minute walk. It's a brisk fall evening and the few trees in the downtown core are beginning to change colour. When Kitty reaches the Four Seasons, she walks into the bar, which is on the street level of the hotel, and looks around. She approaches a woman about her own age sitting alone with a *Toronto Sun* on her table. "Hello, you must be Christie."

"And you must be Kitty." The reporter gets up to shake her hand.

"So you're a reporter. Sounds like an interesting and challenging job. How do you find stories to write about?" A waiter shows up and takes their orders. Christie orders a craft beer while Kitty orders a cosmopolitan.

"Getting back to your question, it depends on your beat. I cover Queen's Park. There are a lot of news releases sent out by the government and I decide if anything is worth following up. Over time, you cultivate your sources. Sometimes people try to pitch a story to you. You just learn to spot a good story over time. It can become pretty routine. It can't possibly be as interesting as being a Muse. It sounds so intriguing. Tell me how you became one."

"I think I was really born to be a Muse. It's just something inside of me. When I was younger, I would tell my friends that I was put on Earth to inspire and help others succeed. They would laugh at me. But I believe it to be true."

"How do you inspire others?"

"You need to understand what a Muse is all about. Muses have been mostly associated with artists but they can be associated with other intellectual pursuits."

"Is it always a woman?"

"Yes and the artist is typically a man though there have been exceptions. Francis Bacon had George Dyer. She is the anima to his animus, the yin to his yang, except that, in a reversal of gender roles, she penetrates or inspires him and he gestates and brings forth, from the womb of the mind."

"It's interesting that you use sexual metaphors. Is sex part of the relationship?"

"There is often a physical side to the relationship to assist with the creative side. However, there are some well-known artists who had no physical relationship with their Muses. Andy

Warhol and Edie Sedgwick. Truman Capote and Babe Paley."

"Well, this is all very informative. Excuse me for asking this: I'm just being curious, of course but you mentioned that you are Rick Tompkins' Muse. Is there a… physical side to your relationship?"

"Unfortunately, there isn't." She has a grin on her face. "It would work so much better if there was."

"I'm sure. Tell me how you met the Minister and how you landed a job in his office. I would think these jobs are hard to come by."

"Umm… we were introduced through a friend. We talked about all different things. He liked the idea of having a Muse. At some point, he thought it would be a good idea for me to join his staff. So the next thing I know, I'm an intern in the government. An unpaid intern."

"Kitty, this has been quite the interesting evening. I am so pleased to have met you and to have gotten an opportunity to chat. I need to be up early in the morning so I will have to call it a night."

"Nice to have gotten to know you as well. Umm… Though I think I may have said too much. I sometimes get carried away."

"No, no. It's all good. I certainly enjoy your openness." With that, Christie gets up and says goodbye. The two women part out on the street and make their way home.

CHAPTER 33

"Half the lies they tell about me aren't true."
Yogi Berra

Lawrence is sitting alone at a table at his local Starbucks, cradling a venti chai tea latte. The cafe has just opened and he and one other customer, a middle-aged man reading a paper, are sitting down. His eyes lock on to the cover of the *Toronto Sun* that the man is reading. The front page has a photo of a woman under the headline and her face looks familiar. Lawrence walks over to the man. "Do you mind if I look at your paper? The person on the cover looks familiar. It looks like someone in my office."

"Sure, go ahead. I was only checking baseball scores from last night."

The photo is of Kitty. Lawrence lets out a gasp when he reads the headline.

TORY MINISTER IN A-MUSING SCANDAL

Rick Tompkins having non-sexual affair with staffer -
EXCLUSIVE PAGE 4

He slumps back into his seat and flips to page 4. There, he finds a full-page article and a previously published photo of the Minister with Brittney and Ginny.

Exclusive Interview with Rick Tompkins' Muse
Christie Lefebre, Queen's Park reporter

Rick Tompkins, Minister responsible for Auto Insurance Reform, has hired a woman to work in his Queen's Park office who claims to also be his Muse. Yes, an honest to goodness Muse. The woman, Katrina Norman, a former Argo cheerleader, goes by the name Kitty and has been in Tompkins' office for several weeks.

Kitty has stated that there is no physical relationship, although she is very candid about her desire to have sex with her boss. She spoke about penetrating his mind and how he would gestate ideas from the womb of the mind.

The Minister and the Muse met several months ago through some mutual friend. It appears that they have been having an affair though to date it has not been sexual. This is not the first time the Minister has been involved in controversy.

During last year's election campaign, he was frequently seen with two young and provocatively dressed women. The Toronto Sun published an exclusive photo of Tompkins and the two women, last November.

In February, Tompkins again ran into hot water when he was turned away from a flight home after a day of meetings in Regina, for being drunk. A video of the altercation at the gate was posted on YouTube.

Following last year's election, Tompkins has been given responsibility for bringing down car insurance rates by 25% in the province. After over a year on the file, no details about how the government plans to bring about such a large rate decrease have been released.

Tompkins and his wife Lois have been married for eighteen years and have two children.

By the time Lawrence is finished reading the article, he is hyperventilating. He grabs his phone and dials Jerry's number.

"Lawrence, it's 6:40. What the fuck is so important?"

"Oh my god! Oh my god!"

"Calm down. What shit is Rick up to now?"

"Did you know that Kitty woman in the office is dating Rick or something like that."

"Where did you get this from?"

"For fuck's sake, it's on the front page of the *Sun*!"

Jerry grabs his tablet and downloads the *Toronto Sun*. "I can't believe this guy. He is truly a moron. I take that back. Even morons are smarter than this. My spit is smarter. A piece of rock is smarter. He is as useless as a baseball pitcher with no arms. Now, I'm going back to sleep and hopefully when I wake up later in the morning, the Premier will have fired him."

"So that's it. You're going to just go back to sleep while our world blows up on us."

"Yup. See you in the office later this morning." Jerry hangs up on Lawrence but he knows he can't go back to sleep. This is the end of the road for Rick and there is a sense of relief knowing that. No more drama. No more damage control. He has been waiting for this cathartic moment. He decides to enjoy the quiet for a few more moments because he knows the rest of the day will be anything but that. Of course, at that very moment his phone chirps. "Oh, hi Mom."

"Good morning Jerry. I hope I'm not disturbing you."

"It's fine, Mom. What can I do for you?"

"I just wanted to pass on some good news to you."

"Great, I could use some good news right now."

"Your cousin Eddie got engaged last night."

"That's great news. I'll have to call him later to congratulate him."

"You know Eddie is six years younger than you."

"Yeah Mom, I know that."

"I wish you could bring me such *nachas*."

"I'm sorry to be such a disappointment to you. I really have to go. I'm going to have a hellish day."

"That's fine. I know my son is too busy for his mother. I'm just happy to have a two minute conversation. You do remember that Jewish New Years starts Thursday evening? I've been cooking all week. I'm making your favorite brisket recipe."

"Yes Mom, I'll be there for dinner on Thursday. I'll talk to you later."

Before he can put down the phone, it chirps again. "Good morning, Geneva."

"Switzer, this is anything but a good morning. I've had a bad feeling about this dickhead from day one. But no one would listen to me."

"Yes, I know."

"A fucking Muse. We have a Cabinet Minister who has a Muse. What's next? Maybe the Finance Minister should get a psychic? You know we all look like a bunch of idiots."

Jerry yawns but covers the phone so that Geneva can't hear it. "I agree this looks very bad."

"Bad doesn't begin to describe it. This may be the worst day of your life. This happened on your watch. You hired a Muse for god's sake!"

"Wait a minute," says Jerry defensively. "I'm tired of you pinning all this guy's shenanigans on me. This has been a total set up. You dumped me in this job and waited for it to blow up in my face. Your office should have fired him long ago. I'm not wearing this."

"Get your ass down here. We need to figure out how to contain this mess. And don't bother suggesting re-releasing that goddamn auto insurance brochure."

He knows that he will have to call Kitty and fire her before she shows up at the office. There will likely be a hoard of reporters waiting at the office and the last thing he needs is for her to be talking to the media again. He realizes her contact information is at the office so he quickly showers and dresses.

On the way to the office, he asks Lawrence to prepare a press release stating that Kitty no longer works in the Minister's office. Jerry sends him a text because he can't stomach the idea of listening to his histrionics over the phone again. He also picks up a copy of the Sun. Maybe he'll get Rick to autograph his copy on his way out to the curb. When he arrives at the office, there is no one in yet and all is still quiet. He knows it won't stay like this for long. He looks up Kitty's number and dials it.

"Hello."

"Hi Kitty, this is Jerry Switzer. Sorry for calling you at home but I needed to reach you right away.

"Okay. Is there a problem?"

"It seems your photo is on the front page of the *Toronto Sun* this morning."

"It is? I'll have to pick up a copy on the way into the office."

"You won't have to come in this morning. You are terminated effective immediately."

He hangs up.

CHAPTER 34

"It's like déjà vu all over again." Yogi Berra

Rick's commute to Queen's Park is like every other morning: slow. His normal routine is coffee in the car and listening to a local sports radio show discussing last night's games. All this while inching his way downtown. His phone rings and the display on his navigation system indicates it's Jerry. "What's up Jerry?"

"You are a jackass!"

"Who do you think you're calling a jackass?"

"If you want to know, why don't you look in your fucking mirror? I just fired your Muse. The two of you are front page news this morning. This place is crawling with media and we're all caught with our pants down."

"How did this happen?"

"Your lady friend talked to your buddy at the Sun, Christie Lefebre. I'm assuming all the nonsense she reported is true. I told you when you raised the issue of an intern that you can't afford to have another thing blow up in your face. But you just don't seem to be able to stay out of trouble. Buddy, you are toast and I'm glad. I'm done cleaning up your messes. They will have you so far up in the backbenches that you'll need binoculars to see the Speaker of the House."

"I don't know..." Before he can finish, Jerry hangs up.

Moments later the phone rings again. It's Kitty. "What the hell did you do?"

"I didn't do anything. I just got a call from Jerry and he fired me." She sounds as if she is crying.

"Oh my god! I told you to be discreet and then you go speak to the media. How stupid can you be?"

"You told me that I shouldn't tell people how we met and instead say we met through a friend. That's what I did. You never said to lie about other stuff."

"So instead you decide to make sure the entire world knows about us by talking to a reporter. Don't you have friends to confide in? What are you doing talking to a reporter?"

"Why are you being such a mean bastard? I didn't know she was going to put that stuff in the newspaper. Why would she do something like that?"

"There is a business concept behind it. Newspapers make money by selling papers. So they like to dig up shit on people. The more shit they dig up, the more papers they sell. You just handed them a latrine full of shit."

He notices there's silence on the other end of the line and realizes that she has hung up on him. His stomach is in knots. How is he going to explain this to Lois? Just then his phone begins to ring again. Of course, it's Lois. "Umm, hi Lois."

"You goddamn asshole! How could you do this to me? You've ruined our lives. Do you realize the whole fucking world is laughing at us?"

"Lois, I can explain..."

"I don't want to hear your bullshit explanation. I've put up with your stupid antics for eighteen years."

"Look there was nothing between us. It was totally innocent."

"You are a fool if you think this is nothing." She is sobbing now. "I'm totally humiliated. What am I going to tell people? My father called to tell me about this. He was livid. He wants me to divorce you."

"Let's talk about it this evening. When we have all calmed down."

"Don't you dare come around here tonight!" The line goes dead. Rick is three for three on hang ups this morning.

At this point, he doesn't really want to go into work but, on the other hand, he can't go back home. He decides it's best to get to the office and assess how much damage has been done by Hurricane Kitty. His train of thought is broken by the sound of his phone ringing. It's his father-in-law. He lets this call go to voicemail. When he receives notification of a message, he reluctantly retrieves it.

"You little prick. You are a disgrace and a loser. I knew this from day one but Lois wouldn't listen to me. It's a little late but maybe she will come to her senses. You are a nothing. I have no interest in what bullshit you have to say. Save it for someone who cares. You are not only an incompetent moron but a philandering idiot to boot. This family is done with you."

So in the past half hour, he has been called a jackass, bastard, asshole, prick, disgrace, loser, moron and idiot. Don made a significant contribution to the list. Quite an accomplishment for just 9:20 in the morning.

Rick parks his car in the underground lot at Ferguson Block and takes the elevator up to his fourth floor office. As the elevator doors open, he is mobbed by a pack of reporters, photographers and cameramen. Reporters are shouting questions. He is blinded by a steady stream of camera flashes. He decides to lower his head and push his way through the corridor to the Secretariat offices muttering "no comment". Once behind locked doors, he relaxes. As he walks towards his own office, he notices people are

263

avoiding making any eye contact with him. When he walks past his secretary Barbara, she doesn't even look up as she informs him he is excused from House duty this morning.

———

Jerry is in the main boardroom in the Premier's Office, fidgeting while waiting for another crisis management meeting to begin. He is fidgeting with his phone. Fidgeting with the file in front of him. Fidgeting with his coffee cup. He has a sense of déjà vu but this is not really déjà vu. More like the movie Groundhog Day: that day that keeps reoccurring over and over again. The usual cast shuffles in and sits down at the table. Everyone is busy looking at their phones. No one speaks.

Finally, Geneva walks into the room. When she sits down, all the phones disappear. "Thank you for clearing your schedules on such short notice. As you all have heard, we have a serious crisis on our hands. The Premier has asked that I gather some views before he makes a decision that is, frankly, pretty obvious. This scandal hurts us for a number of reasons and is offensive to our Conservative base. Let me open it up to the group. Give me your thoughts on how to manage the backlash."

Leslie Geko is first to speak. "It's obvious that the sooner we dump Tompkins, the sooner we can move on. It's still early in our mandate, so we have lots of positive initiatives to come. By the time the next election comes around, this unfortunate mess will hopefully be forgotten."

Lina Nesterov jumps in. "I agree that the best way to handle this is to quickly remove Tompkins and replace him. After that, this will blow over like a typical political scandal where taxpayers' money is not being abused. That is a totally different kettle of fish. I can craft a press release pointing out how Tompkins' behavior does not reflect Conservative Party values and how he breached the public's trust. That sort of stuff."

Geneva doesn't look convinced. "How do we head off the anticipated stories from the other media outlets who were out scooped by the *Sun* and want to catch up by presenting a different angle?"

"The usual way. We limit who can speak on the issue and script them. But that means that this Muse person needs to be muzzled. We don't want her doing further media interviews."

Geneva turns to Jerry. "Jerry, can we keep her quiet?"

"I'm not sure since I was a little rough with her when I terminated her. I can give it a try, though."

Karim Reza joins the discussion. "This in itself wouldn't be so hard to manage if it weren't for the previous incidents. The continuing pattern along with the lack of progress on the file makes us all look incompetent As I see it, damage can be minimized if we could announce a package of reforms that addresses our commitment on this file. But I don't see that happening."

"Well, as it turns out we may catch a break on this file," responds Geneva. "The Insurance Association of Canada and the lawyers who make up the Committee for Fair Auto Insurance have formed some type of coalition. They have presented the Minister with a proposal to bring down rates by ten to twelve percent. This may be the best we can do. I was planning on taking over negotiations with the coalition before the latest crap hit the fan. In light of today's news story, I am making the negotiations a high priority. Jerry and I will meet the group later today. Jerry, you've been pretty quiet. Anything you can add before we break up and I report back to Peter?"

He shifts uncomfortably in his seat. He is still thinking about the plan that the Secretariat is supposed to be coming back to him with. But he feels it is premature to say anything until he has at least seen it. "Nope. I think everyone has already expressed what I'm thinking."

━━━━━━━

Jerry is slumped at his desk trying to motivate himself to get through the pile of work in front of him. He hears a knock at his door and peers up at the intruder. "Yeah, what can I do for you, Rick?"

"I'm in a bit of a jam and have a favour to ask of you."

He can't help but scowl back. "What is it?"

"I need a place to crash tonight."

"You have got to be kidding?"

"I know it's a big favor but it would only be temporary. Things between Lois and I are not so good at the moment."

"Well things between us aren't so good either. But the honest truth is my condo is just 550 square feet. Cozy for one but not big enough for a roommate. You'll be much more comfortable checking into a downtown hotel until you work out your issues."

"I guess you're right."

"It's best that you get yourself a good night's sleep. The next few days here are going to be brutal. To be honest, I don't even see you making it through the week, considering what's going on. But it's not up to me."

Rick pulls up a chair to sit down, which elicits a frown from Jerry. He just wants to be left alone. "I realize I've made some dumb mistakes along the way."

"Now, that's an understatement. I'd say you've made some colossal, career-ending blunders."

"But I really believe in what we're doing here and I think we can eventually achieve our goals."

"But this is politics. You are under a spotlight and there are lots of people just waiting for you to stumble. Your professional life and personal life tend to converge. Social media only accelerates the process." Jerry thinks it might be the right time to prepare Rick for what might be coming. "Maybe you're just not cut out for politics."

"Yeah. Politics is a long ways off from selling insurance."

"It's been a long day. I want to finish getting through a few things still. Why don't you check yourself into a hotel. We'll see what tomorrow brings. But you should prepare yourself for the worst."

"Yep. Thanks for the chat." Rick gets up and walks out the door.

CHAPTER 35

"Wise men talk because they have something to say; fools, because they have to say something." Plato

Rick rolls over onto his back and stares at the ceiling. The sound of traffic in front of the hotel had kept him up much of the night. That and perhaps knowing that his career has plummeted like Enron stock. The blackout curtains swathe the room in darkness with the exception of the clock radio next to the bed and the little bit of light coming from under the door to the hall. Rick stumbles into the bathroom and turns on the light. He shades his eyes until they adjust to the sudden brightness. He notices his head is throbbing and his chest is tight. He hopes that a shower will make him feel better. The water helps to wake him up but Rick's head continues to throb. He had picked up a disposable razor after checking into the hotel the previous evening but has to put on his clothes from the day before. Looking in the mirror, he wonders if people will notice. Today he will have to find time to go to the house and get some clothes.

He is a five minute walk to his office so he decides to get there by foot. It would take longer to get his car out of the hotel garage. When he steps out of the elevator into the hotel lobby, he notices that it is buzzing with activity. He keeps his gaze down, hoping that no one notices him. Outside, it is a warm fall morning which is good because Rick has no coat. He tries to walk briskly but the tightness in his chest is causing him distress and slows him down. By the time he reaches Ferguson Block, his breathing is quite labored, his head is pounding and he is perspiring.

As he walks by Barbara's desk, she supplies her usual greeting. "Good morning Minister. Is there anything I can get you?"

"Morning...yes...some water."

She notices he is red-faced and breathing heavy. "Are you alright?"

"I'm fine...a little out of breath."

She returns moments later with some water and Lawrence. "You look awful," blurts out Lawrence. "What's going on?"

Rick is holding his chest. "Chest pain...hard to breathe."

"Holy crap! You're having a heart attack! Barbara, call 911."

"Noo...."

Lawrence runs around the desk and his large hands loosen Rick's tie. "Hang in there, Minister. Help is on the way."

A short frantic woman with a red hard hat runs into the office. "Don't worry, I've had CPR training."

Lawrence carefully moves Rick onto the floor of his office with his suit jacket under his head. He looks up at the woman in the hard hat. "Who the hell are you?"

"I'm Clarisse, the fourth floor Fire Warden. I'm a first responder."

Moments later, two firefighters and two paramedics dash into the office. One of the paramedics bends down and places a mask over Rick's face. He speaks in a loud voice. "Sir, can you hear me?" Rick nods his head. "My name is Daniel. We are giving you oxygen to help your breathing. We are going to take you to the hospital to get checked out. Do you understand?" Rick nods.

The second paramedic looks up at the three staff standing in the office. "We will need someone to accompany him to the hospital."

Lawrence steps forward. "I'll go with him."

The paramedics walk out to retrieve the stretcher they left outside the office. They wheel it in right next to Rick and carefully lift him up. Once on the stretcher, they use straps to keep him from falling off. One of the firefighters turns to Clarisse. "It looks like we aren't needed here. We're heading out." They walk to the elevator right ahead of Rick and the two paramedics.

Rick's perspective is now a series of ceilings - the corridor, the elevator, the lobby, the ambulance. He sees people passing by trying to make out who is on the stretcher. In the ambulance, he can see that Lawrence has a worried look, as he tightly clutches a chai tea latte. It's cramped in the back of the ambulance because Lawrence's large frame takes up so much space. Fortunately, the ride to Mount Sinai Hospital takes just three minutes. The paramedics pull Rick and the stretcher out of the back of the ambulance and wheel him into the Emergency Department. Lawrence follows behind. One of the paramedics hands some paperwork to one of the triage nurses and returns to the stretcher. He looks down at Rick. "They are going to move you into the first examination cubicle that becomes available." Rick responds by nodding.

Two minutes later a heavy-set nurse in a green outfit appears and pushes the stretcher into a cubicle. She turns to Lawrence. "Are you a family member?"

"No, I'm a work colleague."

"You can wait in the waiting area until he is examined by a doctor." Lawrence nods and walks into a room that is crowded with the ill and injured along with anxious friends and family members. He finds a seat and turns his attention to his cold latte.

The nurse in Rick's examination room hands him a hospital

gown. "Strip down to your underwear and put this on." She walks out and closes the privacy curtains. Once he has changed, she returns and places a blood pressure cuff around his right arm. She then sticks a dozen electrodes connected to an EKG machine to his chest, arms and legs. When she is done the nurse informs him that a doctor will see him shortly. She begins to pull off each electrode, eliciting an "ouch" from Rick as the adhesive on the electrodes removes little patches of body hair. When she is done, she walks out pulling the curtains closed behind her.

Rick's chest is stinging. He wonders how women can endure waxing. Shaving seems more civil. In fact, he wishes the nurse had taken the time to shave him first. He hears muffled voices around him. In the cubicle next to his, he can hear an elderly man repeating, "don't let her near me." He repeats the same line every ten seconds or so. Rick notices the tightness in chest has disappeared. The curtain swings open and a middle-aged doctor walks in. His hair and beard are salt and pepper colored and a pair of reading glasses are perched on the end his nose. "Hello Mr. Tompkins, I'm Dr. Kostopolous. It says on your chart that you're experiencing chest pains. When did they start?"

"This morning when I woke up."

The doctor is looking over Rick's chart. He suddenly looks up. "Aren't you the Minister with the Muse?"

Rick sighs and notices his chest is tightening up again. "Yes."

"Wow! You live an interesting life. Well, I have good news for you Minister. Your heart is just fine."

Rick is clutching his chest again. "Then what's causing my chest pains?"

"I believe they are panic attacks. The symptoms are not unlike cardiac distress. You are obviously under a lot of stress at the moment."

"Yeah maybe. What can I do about it?"

"Obviously, you need to relax. Maybe take some time off. If the symptoms persist then see your family physician who can prescribe some medication to help you cope. I've got to run to check on another patient. You can put your clothes back on. Good luck."

"Come on doc. That's it?" But Dr. Kostopolous has already slipped out of the cubicle. Rick slowly dresses in silence. When he's done, he pulls the curtains and walks into the waiting area.

Lawrence jumps to his feet as Rick approaches. "Oh my god! Are you okay?"

"Grab your purse and let's get the fuck out of here."

Peter Lysiak knows exactly what he will be up against as he takes his seat just prior to the start of Question Period. The Opposition benches are all smiles this morning. Then comes a surprise announcement from the Speaker. "Just before we begin the process of oral question period, I beg the indulgence of the House to allow me to indicate how I intend to proceed with question period. In order to ensure an equitable question period, and one which will permit a maximum number of participants, I will be looking for concise questions and concise answers, and in doing so, I am going to allow approximately one minute for each of the questions. At approximately fifty seconds, I will yell "Question" or "Answer" and you'll have ten seconds, at which time I will rise and the question will be put forward. I am hopeful this will ensure that more members get questions in."

Peter whispers to his Finance Minister, Marco Pinto, who is seated next to him. "There'll be no ragging the puck today. This is going to be brutal."

The Leader of the Opposition asks the first question. "My

first question is for the Premier. For many painful months, you have allowed Minister Rick Tompkins to swing in the wind, and you have refused to accept your responsibility as the ultimate arbiter of your government's standards. In light of the headlines in the *Toronto Sun* yesterday morning, are you going to finally do the right thing, which is to either ask the Minister to resign or fire him?"

The Premier rises to answer the question. "Mr. Speaker, first of all, let me offer my congratulations to you. I don't know if this counts in my minute of response. We wish you well in your deliberations. I personally, and our caucus, pledge our support to you in your endeavor to run this House efficiently. I also want to congratulate the Leader of Her Majesty's official opposition. It will not surprise you that in doing so, I am pleased that he's on the other side of the House and not on this side. Let me say, in response to the question, I have just been made aware of the article around the same time as the Leader of the Opposition. I need to investigate and verify the allegations before taking action."

The Speaker turns to the Leader of the Opposition. "Supplementary question?"

"Yes, Mr. Speaker. How long will it take you to investigate and verify the allegations and finally ask the Minister to resign or fire him? He continues to embarrass the Government and this House. The people of Ontario are waiting for you to do the right thing."

"As I have already stated, I just read the *Sun* article and have not had an opportunity to speak to the Minister regarding the content. It would only be reasonable for that to take place before acting. When that will take place, I can't say at the moment but I don't plan to drag this out."

The Speaker turns to the Opposition. "New question."

The member for York South-Weston rises to ask a question. "It is a shame that the Minister responsible for Auto Insurance Reform isn't present in the House. I would have liked to ask him this question. Due to his absence, I will direct it to the Premier. Yesterday morning's *Toronto Sun* indicates that the Minister avails himself of the services of a Muse. How does the Government use a Muse to develop policy? I look forward to the Premier's answer."

Shouting comes from the Government side of the Chambers. The Speaker rises to his feet. "The member for Renfrew–Nipissing–Pembroke needs to come to order, please. Premier?"

"The member for York South-Weston finds this situation to be humorous. The offices of ministers and members on the Government side are staffed with hard working professionals who put in long hours. If this story is true, it does not reflect the values of the Progressive Conservative Party."

The Speaker looks toward the member for York South-Weston. "Supplementary question?"

"I do have a supplementary question for the Premier. Are there any other muses, psychics, palm readers or clairvoyants working in any of the other ministers' offices?"

At this point, the House erupts with yelling from both sides. The Speaker yells out for order. When the shouting dies down, the Premier responds. "I can assure the House that we will be confirming every appointment in our offices as appropriate professionals. That process will begin today. I am also confident that this is an anomaly and all other staff have necessary experience and skills."

The Speaker recognizes the member for Nickel Belt. "My question is to the Premier. I wonder if you truly understand the significance of the statements you made here in this Legislature several months ago. You provided us with the impression that your Minister responsible for Auto Insurance Reform was hard at work developing a plan for bringing down rates in this province. We now have a Minister who may be out the door and we still have no plan to bring down rates nor an indication on when that plan will be presented to the Legislature. So again, I ask my question. Where is your plan to bring down auto insurance premiums in Ontario and when can my constituents expect to see some savings?"

"Our Government is still committed to bringing forward a plan to provide drivers with premium relief. That commitment isn't dependent on any one individual, not even a Minister. We have a dedicated team working on reforms."

———

Jerry is watching Question Period on television when the Deputy Minister walks into his office. "How is the Premier making out?"

"He is getting hammered, of course." Jerry shuts off the television. "Why don't we get down to business. I can't watch this anymore. Sit down and show me what you have."

"At your request, we further developed our proposal for *The Road Ahead*. I've prepared a preliminary report that is about thirty pages. In addition, I've got a PowerPoint presentation that I can walk you through." She hands him the two documents.

Jerry flips through the slides. "Go ahead."

"Essentially what we have developed is a hybrid system that takes the best of several different models. It takes advantage of the economies of scale that exist when you have a single payer system. But it also preserves the existing competitive marketplace, which benefits consumers by providing lower prices and better service.

Our consulting actuary is suggesting that transactional costs will fall from forty-two percent to just sixteen percent. The average premium paid in the province is $1,500 which means a savings of $390, without touching benefits."

"Our twenty-five percent rate reduction target is $375 which means we would theoretically exceed the target. That's incredible!"

Over the next half hour, Margaret outlines the details of the proposed plan. When she is done, she notices a pained look on Jerry's face. "You don't like it?"

"I think it's great."

"But you don't appear to be that excited. This is the breakthrough the Government has been looking for. If this moves forward, it fulfills a major campaign commitment."

"It's not the plan that I'm thinking about at the moment. It's strictly timing."

"I don't follow you."

"I haven't gotten around to sharing this with you but there is a proposal that has been presented to the government from the insurance industry and the plaintiff bar. The Premier's office has been holding discussions with the two groups. Their proposal will deliver up to twelve percent in savings. It's not close to twenty-five percent, but it has the full support of two major stakeholder groups. That's huge."

"Well, I can see the advantage with going with their plan even if does fall short of the savings the government is looking for."

"But what you have come up with may be superior. For me, this creates a bit of a dilemma. I could sit on your proposed plan for a few weeks and wait for a new minister to be appointed. However, if the discussions with this coalition go too far, then we may lose the opportunity to have the Secretariat's plan considered."

"I agree. This is a tough one."

"In addition, whoever replaces Rick will start their tenure as a Cabinet minister with a bang. But would that be fair? Despite his many missteps and poor judgment, he has also been dogged in trying to deliver on his mandate. I somehow feel he deserves to take the credit. But handing this to him could potentially save his ass. Do we really want that?"

"Jerry, there is no 'we'. I am a public servant and don't wade into the political side of government. You are on your own on this one. I've delivered your plan, you decide who to share it with and when. I will be available to provide technical briefings when needed."

"Yes, I know. I just can't decide which way to go on this one. I think it may be better for everyone if he gets moved out. We all need some stability."

"Well, I'll leave you to think it over."

———

It is late in the day and the sun is barely over the treetops, casting giant shadows over the road. Rick squints when the sun pops out between the trees into his line of vision. He almost misses his driveway while trying to adjust to alternating sun and shadows. He pulls up to the empty space next to Lois' car and walks to the front door. He is about to unlock the door when it swings open. Lois is blocking the doorway, glaring at him. "What are you doing here?"

"I just came to get a few things."

She follows him upstairs into the master bedroom, not saying a word. Rick pulls out a suitcase and a suit bag from his walk-in closet and throws them on the bed. He begins to fill both with socks, underwear, shirts, pants and suits. Out of the bathroom, he brings out a toiletry bag and puts it in the suitcase. All through the packing process, Lois stands silently by the door watching. When Rick begins to zip the bags shut, she finally speaks up. "Do you even know why I'm so upset?'

He stops what he is doing and looks up. "Because I've embarrassed you and your family?"

"No. It's because you had a hidden relationship with another woman. I can deal with all the embarrassing moments. I've been dealing with them for almost twenty years. But now, you've betrayed my trust."

"I'm not having an affair with this woman. Maybe the relationship doesn't make a lot of sense but there was nothing romantic about it."

"That doesn't matter. The fact that you kept it hidden suggests something more disreputable. There is a limit to how much I'll tolerate and perhaps I've now hit that limit. And yes, the fact that this becomes front page news makes it that much worse. It's no longer just about you but now drags me into the picture."

"I swear Lois, I did not mean to hurt you. I made a bad decision. I admit it."

"Rick, I think it's best that you go now." She walks out the door and leaves him alone in the bedroom.

CHAPTER 36

*"Behind every successful man
is a woman, behind her is his wife."*
Groucho Marx

Minister's Muse Fired
Kevin Carter, Toronto Star Queen's Park Bureau Chief

Kitty Norman is now the ex-Muse of Minister Rick Tompkins. She told the Toronto Star that she has been fired from her internship position after another Toronto newspaper published a story linking Norman and Tompkins.

It turns out they have been having a non-sexual affair, clearly an oddity for a political sex scandal in the era of Bill Clinton, Eliot Spitzer and John Edwards. Tompkins met the woman after placing an ad in the strictly platonic personal section of Craigslist. It seems the Minister has old-fashioned morals when it comes to cheating.

The Star caught up with Ms. Norman to find out more about being a Muse. There is no formal training or prerequisite skills needed. "You just decide that's your calling", according to the free-spirited Muse. Muses are notably linked to artists and writers, not politicians. When asked about this, Norman suggested that the creative mind has no boundaries. She noted that Tompkins was involved in a major government review and would benefit from having his creative passion aroused. She confirmed that there was no sex involved in their relationship although she was very open to it and felt it was a very important part of liberating the creative mind.

She noted that most recently, she had been a Muse for the musical director of a symphony. Perhaps Ontario drivers would be paying far less for insurance had she been allowed the opportunity to work her magic. Now we will never know.

Jerry stares at the article on the front page of the *Toronto Star*. Should he even care? This afternoon, Rick is meeting the Premier at which time he will no doubt be removed from Cabinet. Likely, never to be heard from again. Hopefully. Usually these things are done over the phone but Rick's relationship with the Premier has afforded him this additional consideration. His entire tenure as a minister has been a series of 'additional considerations'.

Lawrence pokes his head in Jerry's office. "I see you're looking over that trashy *Star* article. When will this garbage come to an end?"

"Soon enough. The media and public will move on to the next bit of excitement. Maybe the Maple Leafs will fire another coach. Justin Bieber might get into an altercation with some paparazzi. Tim Hortons might increase the price of a cup of coffee by a nickel. They will quickly forget about the Muse."

"So you don't think this new story does more damage?"

"It's really the same story. The *Star* is just trying to catch up to the Sun."

"Well, I'm looking forward to the day when I'll be fielding media calls on auto insurance reforms. I'm heading down to Starbucks for a chai latte. Do you want anything?" He gets up and heads towards the door.

"I'm fine, thanks."

Jerry pulls out his copy of *The Road Ahead* from a desk drawer. He knows that this report will define the legacy of this government. It's that big. Not only that, the minister that tables it in the Legislature will be able to write his own ticket. But it won't be Rick. Although, he knows it should be Rick. Is it right that a new minister walks in the first day on the job and gets handed this report? It would be like a minor league baseball player who gets called up to the majors and handed the MVP award before he even plays a single game. How is that right?

Jerry picks up the report and heads over to Rick's office. He walks right in through the open door and drops the report on Rick's desk. "This is for you."

"What is it?"

"It's *The Road Ahead*. What we've been working on for nearly a year."

"Huh? Where did this come from?"

"Where do you think? It was just delivered by the Secretariat."

Rick is literally wide-eyed staring at the report. "Kinda late now, isn't it? At least for me. I'm out of here in about two hours. Just waiting to head over to Whitney Block for sentencing."

"Well, you have two options. You can leave that on your desk for the next guy. It will make a lovely housewarming gift. On the other hand, you can take it with you and pitch it to Peter. Or maybe you're a fan of the plan being pitched by the insurers and lawyers? In which case, toss it in the trash."

"I still don't see the point of giving it to Peter."

"Well, why don't you take it with you and find out? My opinion is that this is a game changer. Nobody is going to remember embarrassing photos and videos or Muses when this gets released. Like I said, you can hand it to the next minister or you can take credit for the work. Someone on the political side is going to be in the spotlight for the project. It's up to you." As abruptly as he walked into the office, he now turns around and walks out.

With almost two hours to kill before his face-to-face with Peter, Rick decides to flip through the report left by Jerry. Rick is instantly struck by the direction taken in the plan. It never came up in months of consultation with stakeholders. He wonders who actually developed the proposal. He really likes it. He likes it enough to bring it along to show the sheriff before his scheduled hanging.

———

Rick is waiting nervously in the reception area outside of Peter's office in Whitney Block. He looks down at the report in his lap and tries to decide what he plans to say to Peter. Suddenly, the door to Peter's office swings open and out walks Chip Bonham and Graham Wallace. Chip walks over to Rick with his hand extended. "Nice to see you again, Rick."

He is scowling at the two men. "What are you guys doing here?"

"We were just talking about Ex Novo," says Chip.

"So you've gone behind my back and approached the Premier directly?"

Graham smiles back at Rick. "In fact, the Premier invited us in. It was a very productive meeting. Oh, best of luck with your Muse thing!"

Peter's secretary directs Rick into the office. Peter and Geneva are sitting at a table going over some notes. Peter looks up from the file in front of him. "Hi Rick, close the door and have a seat." Rick grabs a chair at the table and sits opposite them. "Rick, we've known each other a long time, which makes this much more difficult for me. I value you as a friend and have backed you up for quite a while but..."

"Sorry to interrupt, Peter. Before you get any further, I think you should take a look at this." He takes the report that has been sitting in his lap and tosses it across the table.

Peter picks up the document. "What is this?"

"*The Road Ahead*. Delivered as promised."

Geneva looks at him suspiciously. "Where did this come from?"

"Where do you think? That's what you asked me to work on for the past year."

Peter spends about ten minutes skimming through the document. He then hands it over to Geneva. Rick sits silently as they go through it. When Geneva has finished going over the document, Peter takes back the report from her. "What do you think?"

"We need to verify the numbers in the report but I have to admit, I like it."

"Me too. Good work, Rick. No, great work really." He sighs. "As you likely know, the purpose of this meeting was to inform you that I was going to remove you from Cabinet. In light of what we have here, that would be unjust."

Geneva objects. "Can we realistically have him continue in light of these outrageous news stories? And what are you going to tell the coalition about their plan?"

"Geneva, you know this is a much better proposal than what the insurers and lawyers brought us. This is what drivers are expecting from us. The news stories will die off. Even more quickly after Rick delivers this report to the Legislature. Geneva, we need the communications people to begin work immediately on a communication plan around the launch of *The Road Ahead*."

Rick breaks out in a big smile. "Thanks Peter, for having faith in me. But really folks, have I ever let you guys down?"

Geneva is shaking her head. "Let's not go there. You pulled a rabbit out of your hat this time. Next time you might not be so lucky."

Peter agrees. "Let's get away from all the drama from now on."

———

Rick and Lois sit in a booth in the back of an Italian restaurant in a Woodbridge strip mall. The restaurant looks like almost every other Woodbridge Italian restaurant with dark wood paneling, Roman arches and staff carrying oversized pepper grinders. The food portions are huge and the recipes were handed down from *nonna*. It is a Tuesday night and most of the tables are empty.

Rick is staring down at his glass of wine, nervously playing with the stem. Lois is looking at him, trying to make eye contact. "Aren't you curious about what I wanted to speak to you about?"

"Well, I'm more worried than curious."

"You should be worried. You've been a first-class jackass. I'm embarrassed to leave the house with all the newspaper stories about us."

"I know... I've been selfish and foolish."

"I need to know. Did you have an affair with that woman?"

"No. Even the newspaper articles confirm that."

"Weren't you the one who told me that the newspapers always get it wrong?"

"Yes. But this is one of those situations where they actually got it right."

"I've given this a lot of thought. I'm not sure you fully understand how wrong it is to maintain a hidden relationship, even if it is platonic. I've always trusted you but I'm not sure if I can trust you anymore. However, I'm willing to give you a chance to win back that trust. That's my best offer."

"That's a damn good offer. Not one I'm going to turn down. Nothing like this is going to ever happen again. I've learned a good lesson here."

"Don't make me any promises. You've had your one chance. Don't blow it."

"I won't."

"You can move out of whatever dump you're in and move back into the house."

CHAPTER 37

"It ain't over till it's over." Yogi Berra

Jerry and Geneva search around the gallery of the Legislative Chamber for two empty seats. It is nearly filled to capacity as a result of the media advisory that was issued by the Premier's Office. The advisory merely stated that Rick Tompkins, Minister responsible for Auto Insurance Reform will be making an important announcement in the Legislature. Considering the drama that has been taking place for much of the past week, it has brought out a mob of reporters. They find two seats together and sit through Question Period until it is time for Members' Statements.

Jerry whispers to Geneva. "Interesting crowd. This is not your typical Queen's Park press gallery crowd."

"Our communications people have been fielding dozens of calls. You know how we often leak the news to our preferred outlets? Well, on this one we haven't told a soul. No one is sure what's coming."

When it's time for Members' Statements, the Speaker recognizes Rick who rises to read his statement, prepared by the Premier's Office.

"Mr. Speaker, I am pleased to advise the members that I am

tabling a report entitled *The Road Ahead* which will enable this Government to reduce auto insurance premiums on average by twenty-five percent. This report honours the commitments we made last year, commitments to provide fair and affordable auto insurance. Today, we are delivering on those promises.

"Mr. Speaker, today we are beginning the process to transform an expensive and confusing auto insurance scheme into a fair and cost efficient one — a system that will be unique in North America. The reforms outlined in *The Road Ahead* will make insurance premiums more affordable, make insurance more available and provide reasonable and fair compensation for everyone. On a future date, we will be introducing legislation that will reflect the system outlined in our plan.

"Mr. Speaker, the former government did many grave injustices to Ontario motorists, while delivering windfall profits and incomes to insurance companies, lawyers and rehabilitation providers. Our reform package is the result of an auto insurance review that has lasted for over a year. Throughout this period, we have encouraged widespread participation. The resulting dialogue involved hundreds of individuals and interest groups. Strong arguments supported a range of often conflicting positions. We believe that these reforms will achieve fairness and the best possible balancing of these diverse objectives Most importantly, they will make it more affordable to own a car in Ontario. Thank you, Mr. Speaker."

As he takes his seat, the Government side of the House breaks out in applause and desk banging, as the Speaker attempts to resume order and move on to the next member scheduled to make a statement. The media have been handed copies of the statement and are busy preparing questions for the media scrum that will form once the day's session ends. Jerry notices that Geneva is actually beaming, which is a rare occurrence. They get up and follow the media out in anticipation of Rick's exit from the Chambers. As they walk down the stairs, Geneva comments, "So far so good. Let's see how we make out when the questions start flying."

She is right. It's a little like the moment the gate drops and the bulls are let loose in Pamplona. The shouting. The madness. People being trampled underfoot. Reporters actually have to bellow and shout above their colleagues to have their question heard. As they reach the doors leading to the Chambers, they swing open and Rick briskly marches to the awaiting mob with microphones and cell phones shoved in his face.

"Minister, how soon will you be introducing legislation?"

Rick stops to respond. "The Government plans to introduce a bill to bring about the proposed reforms in *The Road Ahead* in a few weeks. It's a challenging agenda but Ontario drivers desperately need rate relief."

"Minister, will you continue to be responsible for leading reforms? Rumour has it that you are on your way out."

"The Premier has assured me that I will be in charge of seeing this reform package through the Legislature. He has stated that there are no plans to replace me. I'm looking forward to the challenge."

"Minister, when can Ontario drivers expect to see their rates go down?"

"We expect to push our legislative package through the House as quickly as possible. Hopefully, the Opposition won't be using procedural tactics to slow down passage of our bill. With their cooperation, we can deliver lower premiums in a few months."

He notices *Sun* reporter Christie Lefebre pushing forward through the crowd holding her phone in her outstretched hand to record the questions and answers. As she approaches Rick, she shouts out, "Minister, the public is interested in knowing how much of a role your Muse had in the package of reforms you've just announced!"

Rick walks past her without responding. The surging mob closes in behind him and Christie's phone is knocked out of her hand. The phone is trampled like a fallen runner at Pamplona, as she looks on helplessly.

"Minister, does the insurance industry support your reform package?"

Geneva and Jerry hang back, taking it all in. Rick is easily handling the questions thrown his way. "Well Jerry, looks like your guy has been able to learn a few tricks after all. So are you ready to leave the circus and join us at Whitney Block?"

"What are you offering?"

"Deputy chief of staff. You would be my second in command. You deserve it."

"Seriously? That is quite the offer. Can I sleep on it?"

"Of course. Let's meet for breakfast on Friday morning and we can talk about it some more."

"All right. 7:30 at Fran's?"

"Okay. See you then."

━━━━━━━━━━

Ameena 3 has arrived a little early for her weekly constituency meeting with Rick. She drops in to visit Jerry, who is reviewing the morning's news clippings. "Hey Jerry! How's it going?"

"You know how it is around here. One day, they're getting the guillotine ready for you. The next day, they're planning a parade in your honor."

"I see you are going through the clippings. The media coverage is incredibly positive. So I guess he isn't going to be dumped any time soon."

Before Jerry can respond, Rick bounds into his office. "Hey Jerry. What is it you people say? Mazel Tov? It feels good to be me this morning."

"I bet it does."

"All those people who doubted I could find twenty-five percent savings, what do they have to say for themselves now?" He has a smirk on his face that Jerry would like to knock off with a two-by-four.

"Really? So tell me how you came up with those savings?"

"You know I don't have to come up with all the ideas myself. That's why we employ all those smart people."

"While those smart people are plugging away, you spend your time stepping into piles of dog shit. Then those smart people have to keep cleaning you up. Just so you can step into another pile."

"What the fuck is up with you today? You need an attitude adjustment if you want to be working around here. Remember, we're on the fast track buddy. Hey #3, what are all the brown people in the riding up to?"

"You mean all those nice people in the riding who voted for you? We have some issues that we need to discuss."

"Follow me into my office. We'll leave Mr. Grumpy to go over my press clippings. He's probably sore that the papers don't mention my loyal executive assistant."

Jerry is about to say something but before he can get it out, they are gone. Right now, he's looking forward to the moment when he tells Rick that he's leaving. That'll remove the smirk from his face. Implementing a package of complicated reforms is not going to be a walk in the park. Rick is going to need a lot of hand holding to pull it off. But it will be someone else holding the leash.

When Jerry arrives at the diner on Friday morning, Geneva is already at a booth draining a cup of coffee. Above her is a bright red neon sign declaring 'Welcome Home to Fran's'. He slides into the seat opposite her. "Good morning. Sorry I'm late."

A waiter approaches with a pot of coffee. "Are you having coffee?"

"Yes, thank you."

He fills his mug. "Do you need more time to order?"

"Go ahead, Geneva."

"I'll have a vegetarian omelet."

"Just bring me a toasted bagel."

"Jerry, you're late as usual. You may have been able to slack off in the Minister's office but you can't be pulling that kind of stuff in the Premier's Office."

"Umm. I'm not coming to the Premier's Office."

"What? Don't tell me you've decided to stay with Minister Bumfuck?"

"No. I've decided I'm leaving government."

"Are you serious?"

"I am. I've had enough of 90-hour workweeks. My sleep interrupted for a response to the latest crisis that everyone will forget about in twenty-four hours. The spin-doctors trying to convince you that shit smells good. Politicians who think they walk on water but actually are waist deep in manure. Boiling down complex issues into a two-page briefing note. The Queen's Park press running around looking for any lame story to throw together in time for their filing deadline. Throne speeches with unattainable goals. I'm tired of it all."

"I can't believe what I'm hearing. This is your life. I think you just need some time off."

"Maybe. But I still think it's time to do something different."

"Like what?"

"I'm thinking about writing a book. Maybe I'll write about all this. I haven't decided."

She laughs. "You write about that night at my place when I was drunk and, so help me god, I will hunt you down and cut off your balls."

"I'm glad to see how you've been able to move on from that night."

"Look, I hope you know what you're doing."

"No, I don't but I do know that I don't want to do this anymore."

"Too bad. I was looking forward to having you back on the team." The waiter brings them their food. Geneva looks over at his bagel. "I can tell you one thing I wasn't looking forward to. All the poppy seeds around the office from your stupid bagels."

———

Jerry and Ameena 3 are trying to coordinate packing and unpacking. As Jerry empties a desk drawer into a box, Ameena 3 empties one of her boxes into the drawer. She turns to him. "I still can't believe you are leaving. Not just this job. But government altogether. How do you feel about it?"

"It feels strange. But I also feel liberated."

"Any last minute advice for the incoming executive assistant?"

"Expect the worse and you won't be disappointed."

She laughs. "I know it can't be that bad. I ran his constituency office so I know what he's like."

"You'll be fine."

Lawrence strolls into the office. "Good, I caught you before you left. I wanted to say a final goodbye."

"It's not like I'm leaving the continent. I still live a few blocks away."

"Yeah, we know but you aren't going to be around the office anymore. Hey, I also meant to show you guys a news article I noticed this morning."

"Sure. Let's have it."

"I'll read it to you: 'The Minister's Muse Is On The Move. Kitty Norman, the notorious Muse who once worked for Ontario Minister Rick Tompkins, has a new assignment. After being fired by the Minister, Kitty was flooded with hundreds of offers for her Muse services. The offers came from painters, writers, businessmen and musicians. She finally accepted an offer from an unnamed hockey player on the Edmonton Oilers. She has since moved to the city of Edmonton to join him. It seems you can't keep a good Muse down'."

ACKNOWLEDGEMENTS

Writing would be such a solitary endeavor without a Muse. Who else would keep you company late at night, provide inspiration when your creativity begins to flag, and lie by telling you how wonderful you are? At one level, you seem like a figment of my imagination and don't exist. At another level, you are very real and vital to my creative endeavor. Without you, would I have any creative power? How could I fail to acknowledge your existence? So thank you.

There are so many people to thank. A first time author needs a long and extensive support group to take on such a daunting venture. It was several months before I even revealed to people that I was writing this novel, because I didn't believe in myself. When I did acknowledge what I was undertaking, the support and encouragement was overwhelming. I'll be forever grateful to my family, in particular, my wife, Mary Anne. Whenever I doubted myself, she assured me that I wasn't wasting my time.

Thanks to Chantal Saville and Deb Smythe for being such wonderful and encouraging sounding boards. You are both very gifted and funny writers. I look forward to our monthly get-togethers to talk about our work over a glass of wine. In particular, I am indebted to Chantal for passing on her knowledge of social media, publishing and editing. Also, Sarah Messina, who helped me publish this novel.

I also owe a special thank you to Kathy Kruk, who is a great friend and an avid reader. She insisted that I share my draft manuscript with her book club and we had a wonderful evening discussing The Road Ahead. Thank you to John Kruk, Shannon Matthews, Victoria Matiash, Larry Wilson, Marilyn Stanley, Lee Coplan, Caroline Magpie Jones, Erin Woods, Daniel Iggers and Daniella Laise for your interest and support. I know there were others, as well, who took the time to read drafts and provide encouragement and valuable feedback. So many contributed to this book.

I also want to acknowledge two outstanding novelists, Terry Fallis and Michelle Berry, who take time from their busy schedule to teach novice writers, such as myself.

Finally, I want to recognize my parents, Ela and Shifra Handler. They struggled so that I might be able to succeed in life. They would have been so proud.

W.H.
Toronto, 2016

ABOUT THE AUTHOR

WILLIE HANDLER grew up in Toronto and did his undergraduate work at the University of Toronto. He also has graduate degrees from the Schulich School of Business at York University in Toronto and the Fox School of Business at Temple University in Philadelphia, Pennsylvania. He spent over thirty years in various positions in the Ontario public service. before leaving in 2011. Much of his time in government was spent on auto insurance regulatory policy. He also operates a consulting practice. He currently lives in Thornhill with his wife and blogs at www.williehandler.com. Follow @WillieHandler on Twitter.